The Essence of Production

An introduction for the student
and the general reader

Also available in this series

CONDITIONS OF SALE

Management Series

The Essence of Production

An introduction for the student
and the general reader

P. H. LOWE

A Pan Original

PAN BOOKS LTD · LONDON

First published 1970 by Pan Books Ltd,
33 Tothill Street, London, S.W.1

330 02510 4

Printed in Great Britain by
Richard Clay (The Chaucer Press), Ltd.,
Bungay, Suffolk

Contents

Preface

The subject of production covers a wide field. Its many facets tend to confuse the layman and, as it is an applied, vocational subject, it contains much material, drawn from a variety of sources. To gather all that is relevant into one publication may well lead to a 1,000-page handbook, filled with details and techniques. Such an approach may not, however, provide an overall perspective, and the reader might be tempted to leave production to the practitioners. Alternatively, a separate study of some of the constituent topics may lead to better understanding, but in a more limited context.

There is a case for the general introduction of production which indicates its ramifications as a subject, its diversities and problems, without the sacrifice of the total view. Equally, there is the need to integrate its various components, so that these may be seen within the general framework of business management and in relation to other functional business activities. The book, therefore, is a first step to those who wish to acquaint themselves with production, whether they are within or outside industry. For those who wish to inquire more deeply into the subject, references and further reading suggestions are provided at the end of the appropriate chapter.

The reader will note the general descriptive approach of the book. Description often tempts prescription; perhaps the temptation has not been completely resisted, but there is certainly no attempt to advise on, let alone solve, some of our complex industrial problems. The general public needs to know more about the principles and problems of production if it wishes for a fuller understanding of our present industrial situation. It is this fuller understanding, rather than specialist knowledge, which this book endeavours to provide.

While much of the general setting is in terms of organization and economic appraisal, Chapters Four and Six introduce a more technical background. It is hoped that the approach and treatment does not put this beyond the interest of the general reader; in any case, much of what has been written, in such a context, is self-evident on reflection. Production and technology are linked; the organization of production would remain an unreal abstraction if no reference were made to the setting in which it takes place.

London   *December 1968*

The Essence of Production

An introduction for the student
and the general reader

CHAPTER ONE

The Meaning of Production

1 THE NEED FOR ANALYSIS

Since 1945 there has been a continuous growth of interest in the field of management and business studies. On the whole, the growth has been quite vigorous and does not seem to have been impeded by the occasional doubt as to the precise meaning of these studies and their extent.

Although the association may not be immediately apparent, this growing emphasis, particularly on management studies, reflects some aspects of deeper social, political, and economic changes. These changes are by no means confined to the United Kingdom, and parallel developments may be traced in Western Europe, the communist countries, Japan, and the United States. The scale of change may vary as a function of social and political institutions, but the trends are in the same direction.

The lesson of 1945 and the Second World War was the ultimate importance of economic power to sustain military operations. When Churchill claimed that the real victory was snatched from the Germans in 1940 at Dunkirk he could make this claim despite unprecedented losses of armour and equipment. These could more easily be replaced than trained fighting manpower. As long as the war effort and production could develop, as long as the war economy remained intact, there was hope about the ultimate outcome despite the heavy scale of material losses. Subsequently, when the Atlantic Alliance took shape there was every reason for these hopes to grow because the United States economy, with its unrivalled production facilities and potential, had now become available for the common cause. Economic strength had become a basic factor in the waging of total war. Furthermore, when all the resources of a country were to be mobilized the physical size of these resources and their utilization became important. The effective utilization of a country's resources was, in turn, viewed as a function of its technological attainments, both in terms of research and development as well as in proved production processes. With political and economic strength acknowledged as an important constituent of political power and influence, political awareness fostered deeper interest in the working of the economy and the performance of its industrial sector. The decline of the United Kingdom's political standing in the world, coupled with the contraction of overseas military commitments, seemed to correlate with a relatively weaker economic position.

In contrast to the fears about our external economic standing, there has been a domestic preoccupation with the material standards of living. The preoccupation has been more with the precise level of such standards rather than their foundation. While throughout history the general level of prosperity had always been of special interest to the middle and commercial classes, it seemed now to be of definite concern to all sectors of society.

This increasing emphasis on the material aspects of human well-being – as if man no longer had a soul – seems to reflect the decline of religious and social values, which, in turn, affect the attitude to work and the rewards or satisfaction that might flow from it. Work itself, on the factory shop floor, so often fragmented, monotonous, and unable to make appropriate use of the products of the most developed and expensive system of education in history, may well cause this reaction: that if there can be no work satisfaction, then let at least the material reward be as high as possible. The outside world, represented by the cinema, television, press, and reinforced by the easier opportunities for mass foreign travel, has stressed the comforts of material well-being. Full employment, together with relatively cheap food and consumer durables, has tended to confirm this. The next world seems a long way off; the comforts of this world are tangible and close at hand.

The preoccupation with material well-being has found expression in political thought. Views as to the appropriate role of government reflect the concept of the 'Welfare State'. In discussion, the Government is likened to the board of a large business corporation: it is assessed in terms of 'efficiency', on its capacity for forward planning, and on its ability to develop policies which foster the material advancement of the country. There is little doubt that the view of the State as the main tool of planning and economic development – as portrayed in communist countries – has had an influence on public outlook. If in these countries ultimate material success endorses the concentration on the secular, material aspects of life, then the appeal of such philosophies could well grow.

One of the problems of the welfare state is that it is not quite sure about the actual amounts of welfare it provides. The costs may be readily assessable, but the precise benefits cannot be so easily quantified. Adding up the utilities of welfare schemes and social legislation is a somewhat hazardous calculation. Specialists, such as sociologists, welfare economists, econometricians, and statisticians, have come to the rescue; and a most significant development in the machinery of government has been the growth of such advisory and specialist staff groups. To provide some of the raw material for policy discussion in a modern industrial society, there is a need to measure, quantify, to simulate, and to construct models for the purpose of prediction. The specialist finds opportunity here for the exercise of his skills. But he brings to his tasks not only his professional training and experience but also his assumptions and presumptions, his views about society, whether implicit or explicit, as well as his culture patterns. The climate of opinion with which such specialist skills are associated might well be discounted, but this may not prevent it from subconsciously permeating to the policy-making level. There has been a natural reflection of such trends in the establishment over the last few years of bodies such as the Ministry of Technology, the National Economic Development Council (NEDC), the Department of Economic Affairs, the National Board for Prices and Incomes, etc.

There is now considerable public discussion about problems of national economic growth, improvements in productivity, economic efficiency, and industrial competitiveness in international markets. The economists and financial journalists are joined by cabinet ministers and Members of Parliament in stressing the need for improvement in this field. The taxpayer is made continuously aware (by consecutive budget measures) that there are national economic problems, even if in his own personal setting they do not seem to be very apparent. We are continuously told that our wealth (expressed in the national product per head) is growing more slowly than the wealth of other countries; that the relative advantages which we once possessed as a trading and industrial nation have been whittled away and lost; that in relation to countries such as Western Germany and Japan 'we are losing the race'. In the terminology of football, we are informed that we may be relegated from the first division of economic status, unless we work harder or are more receptive to new ideas, etc.

The relative growth of wealth of some of the more important industrial countries is given below. The information is taken from the November 1968 issue of the *Monthly Bulletin of Statistics*, issued by the Statistical Office of the United Nations. The index numbers of industrial production form a useful indicator for the purpose of such a comparison.

While the rate of growth does not, of course, reflect absolute levels, the performances of the United States, Canada, and Sweden are particularly noteworthy, when considering their national product per head and the standard of living already achieved by these countries.

The role of economic strength in the status of a country has been briefly indicated. In war, in support of military operations, in peace, as a determinant of the standard of

INDEX OF INDUSTRIAL PRODUCTION
1963 = 100

Country	1960	1967
Belgium	83	112
Canada	83	130
Czechoslovakia	87	129
West Germany	88	114
Italy	77	128
Japan	70	162
Netherlands	87	129
Sweden	83	126
USSR	77	139
United Kingdom	95	112
United States	87	127

living – it remains an inherent factor of national well-being. Economic strength in turn is a function of the capacity to produce wealth, ie, the capacity to produce goods and services which have value because there is an effective demand for them. The availability of goods and services at the place of demand is, of course, more than a matter of mere production; it also involves marketing and distribution. Nevertheless, whatever the importance of marketing in a given field, the goods for sale remain a function of production.

A well-known soluble-coffee manufacturer recently launched a new brand of instant coffee. The product, breaking new ground in customer appeal, was heavily promoted and initial demand was growing rapidly. A production failure caused an extended plant shutdown – the shelves stayed empty; an opportunity was lost. The demand existed, but the actual sales were not commensurate with the costs of the product launch.

Effectiveness in production is as important to company or industrial well-being as it is to the general standard of living. Its twin basis, technological and organizational competence, provides the setting. On it depends the direct livelihood of about 8,500,000 people in the manufacturing industries, which with their dependants form about 35–40 per cent of the total population. As secondary employment also depends on this industrial effectiveness, the implications on the national welfare are, of course, greater than these figures suggest.

2 THE CONCEPT OF PRODUCTION

Production concerns itself with the creation of all goods and many services, be they such diverse items as steam turbines, furniture suites, or laundry facilities. Creation includes the modification and assembly of goods already in existence, such as the use of copper wire for the winding of electric motors, the printing and cutting of newsprint to produce a newspaper, or the assembly of a television set from bought-out components. It may also include the repair and servicing of existing goods. In a strict sense, agricultural production would also be relevant here, but it is proposed to confine the discussion to industrial production. The context is the factory – as defined in the Factories Act 1961 – where buildings, plant, equipment, materials, and people are brought together on to specific sites to achieve this physical creation of goods and services, within an integrated system of organization. In this sense one can also differentiate between those service industries which would be covered by such a context and those which would fall outside; although it might not always be easy to draw a fine dividing line. An industrial dry-cleaning plant would come under this heading, but what if the dry-cleaning service is provided in a shop with a backroom? The definition of a factory is by no means always clear, as was seen recently in the House of Lords judgement (J. & F. Stone Lighting & Radio Ltd versus Haygarth – October 1966) that a backroom to a radio shop, used for the servicing of television sets, constituted a factory in law.

The manner in which production takes place and the various facets of its organization are of interest to a number of specialist observers. The engineer, particularly the production technologist, is concerned with production methods and processes; the type of plant used; how it is interrelated and what skills are required for its operation. He is also interested in the type of power or services needed by such plant, its maintenance and building requirements. On the other hand, the administrator is concerned with the type of organization which is most relevant to plant operations, the manner of control, and how decisions are made. Matters of plant utilization, shift work, resource inputs and allocation, costs, productivity, factor substitution, and many other related topics engage the attention of the industrial economist. Similarly, the social scientists are concerned with the relationships of people within the factory setting; how individuals and groups react to one another and how they respond to work tasks, the formal organization and management policies.

Most of the literature concerned with matters of production is written in the context of just such a specialist approach. This is not surprising, because the subject is vast, and a discussion or book tends to become somewhat unmanageable if all the aspects of production are covered in some detail. The consequence of this is a loss of overall view or perspective of what production is all about. A collection of fragments does not make the whole. The interrelationships of the various constituents which make a production unit a living, organic being tend to be underestimated as a result. This is of particular significance when the dynamic setting of such an organization is considered. How does the unit adapt itself to change? What problems are caused? What tensions develop? What is the nature of human resistance? How are such difficulties overcome? The answers require specific studies in depth, carried out in an evaluated context. Such specialist contributions, however, need the framework of an overall vision. While the number of relevant specialist studies, for instance in the social sciences, is rapidly increasing – see, typically, Lupton's account[1] – there are relatively few examples of wider studies in a total company context. Perhaps the most notable example here is the Glacier Project[2], where one of the most prominent students and observers was at that time both Chairman and Managing Director of the Glacier Metal Co Ltd and therefore uniquely placed to obtain a total view.

It is also clear from simple observation that there is a wide range of industries, employing a great variety of production processes, some of which are very specialized in their nature. Each type of production unit will require its specialists. This is necessary for competence in the control and organization of specific manufacturing activities. For instance, part of the job requirements for a production manager in a paper mill may be thorough training in papermaking science. Similarly, it may again be part of the requirements for a workshop superintendent to have served an engineering apprenticeship. Such specialist training and experience must, however, be supplemented before success in a position of responsibility for production can be assured. The operation of manufacturing units in a competitive situation requires the knowledge and application of basic principles of production organization and management. It is interesting to note that specialist requirements, although important for the industry concerned, may be of limited transfer value. Typically a degree in paper-making science and plant experience in a paper mill may be of little value in a glass factory. On the other hand, basic knowledge of production organization and quality control, for instance, can be of equal value in such a different context.

Developing the argument further, effectiveness in a position of production responsibility may require among other things:

a   Broad and relevant background. This may be largely covered by technical or professional training.

b   Specialist knowledge and experience required for specific production processes. Training here is usually within the industry concerned, alongside the processes and techniques involved.

c   Knowledge of the principles of production organization and management.

A general review of the principles of production organization (*c*) is the purpose of this book. These principles become of relatively greater importance as the size of the production unit and its complexity increases. They also acquire greater prominence when the responsibility for production is at a higher level within an organization. These production organization principles constitute in a sense a common link which traverses the specialist technologies of different industries, and become part of a sound production background. That this is so may be noted from current advertisements for many senior production and management appointments, as well as for management consultants specializing in production problems. The skills and experience of managing production – in a line appointment – together with sound knowledge of the techniques of planning and control, in a manufacturing context, are the qualities most sought after. Specialist technological experience is in most cases a subsidiary point. In some cases too much of this may well be regarded as a disadvantage.

The range of subject matter, relevant to the study of production organization, can broadly be described as follows:

a   The study of new product development and design, with particular reference to production feasibility.

b   The planning of production from global considerations, such as the building of new factories, right through to detailed specification work relating to individual production operations.

c   The nature of production processes, their manner of operation, based on manual or automatic control.

d   Product quality. The setting of standards and techniques of measurement.

e   The provision of production services and building facilities.

f   Production control. The preparation of production schedules and the organization required to achieve these.

g   The human aspects of production.

h   The management of production, with particular reference to the organizational structure of various types of production units.

i The economics of production.

j The effectiveness of production. The manner in which production performance can be specified and measured.

The substance of these related fields of interest will be described in the chapters which follow. But, before doing so, it will be desirable to discuss some of the implications of the range of material put forward.

3 THE CONTEXT OF PRODUCTION STUDIES

The range of material that will be described has a substantial vocational bias. It reflects the economic need for trained managerial manpower in the manufacturing industries. Knowledge and techniques are not put forward for their own sake: they must be relevant to the industrial context. As the range of subject matter is in an academic sense inter-disciplinary, most of the present and potential managers of production are unlikely to be equipped with such a width of background; unless, of course, they have made an explicit effort to widen their interests. From general observation, this often has to be a spare-time activity and is usually confined to a persevering minority. Formal education, on the whole, is not geared to such a vocational spectrum of subject matter, not even at the technical college or the technological university level. Admittedly, a good segment may be covered either in a technological or social science context, but when the limits of one of these broad fields are crossed to go to the other – even if a syllabus provides for it – the thinking is not integrated and the teaching approach tends to ignore the interrelations of the various subjects in a production setting.

In broad terms, the graduate or his professional equivalent who embarks on a career in production is essentially a specialist in training and outlook. In many cases the specialism may be only of limited relevance to the field of production. Granted that what industry needs is the 'trained mind', perhaps even irrespective of the context in which this training was attained. It may be argued, however, that the trained mind, by itself, is inadequate; with it must come an appropriate outlook and some judgement. These could be better developed by a form of education that is more in harmony with the spectrum of subject matter relevant to production. In a sense, preparation for competence in production management is, in principle, not unlike medical training, where the ultimate professional purpose of training is well understood; yet this does not prevent the future doctor getting his knowledge from a wide range of basic subjects.

Essentially, production draws much of its subject matter from the following fields:

a The behavioural sciences, such as sociology, social anthropology, psychology.
b Physiology, as associated with ergonomics – the study of man – machine/environment relationships.
c Cybernetics, the study of control systems, both in an organizational and in an engineering sense.
d Mechanical engineering.
e Electrical engineering, including electronics.
f Workshop practice.
g Statistical analysis.
h Economics.
i Accounting practice.
j Management principles and practice.

Of course, both mechanical and electrical engineering are associated with more fundamental studies in science, particularly physics.

The vocational emphasis of the subjects within the scope of production organization, as already defined, entails an interdisciplinary approach in an academic sense. From the point of view of educational administration this raises a number of problems which stem from the accepted divisions of knowledge for the purpose of teaching and research. Of course, the division of labour for the pursuit of knowledge makes sense. Where there seems to be an infinite horizon

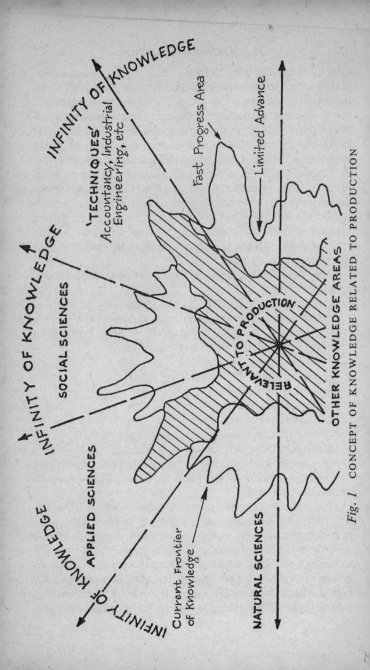

Fig. 1 CONCEPT OF KNOWLEDGE RELATED TO PRODUCTION

after a certain limited stage of knowledge has been reached, then specialization is likely to be the most effective way of making further consistent progress. This does not rule out significant advances made by brilliant amateurs in a specialized field – nevertheless, the knowledge, techniques, and equipment, particularly for scientific research, are becoming so refined and complex that such occurrences may be increasingly rare in the future. There is therefore an association between success and specialization in science. To the scientific mind, however, this tends to lessen the attractiveness of interdisciplinary training. There are other and deeper problems associated with the organization of knowledge, and these may perhaps be better visualized by the foregoing diagram.

The characteristics of much of the scientific work today are sophistication, and a specialization often so intense that it is more akin to fragmentation. The frontiers of knowledge and understanding may often be far forward, and it is difficult to foretell where and when the value of application will arise in a production context. What will be of practical, economic value may be pedestrian in a scientific sense, at least to the research workers in that particular field. Nevertheless, the rate of industrial technological change has been accelerating, particularly in the larger, more technologically based companies, such as the electronic, petrochemical, and drug industries, etc. For instance, the amount of scientific knowledge and technological attainment incorporated in modern process industry is impressive by any standard. Here at least one can perhaps relate a production situation to a scientific environment. In some cases plant and equipment may be at the very limit of knowledge, particularly where production problems have initiated research work. Yet, in other cases plant and equipment may look primitive in a strict scientific sense and may reflect essentially the product of craft ingenuity. In any one given production situation, plant could be distributed on a scale and vary quite widely between such extremes. The newer technological industries have much of their plant at one end of the scale, while the old-established 'craft' industries have a bias towards the other end.

Again, much of the subject matter that is of interest to the manager in production is associated with the social sciences. This is particularly the case where the labour content in manufacture is high and the labour force is substantial. However, the differences between the natural sciences and the social sciences cause problems to many who have largely developed in only one of these two fields. To the technologist much of what the social scientist has to offer seems ragged and confusing. He is bewildered by some of the acrimony shown in debate between different schools of thought, often on matters which to him look self-evident. The data and raw material for theory development often lacks the crispness to which he is accustomed. The social sciences are concerned with the actions and behaviour of man; he presumes – as a sample of the species – that his personal experiences entitle him to extrapolate with equal confidence. The social scientist, on the other hand, mistrusts the uniformity of much of the scientific thinking, at least at the level at which he might meet it as a layman. The 'single solution' type of problem looks artificial to him. Whereas the technologist, as a human being, cannot help but know a little about the subject matter of the social sciences, technology to the social scientist is often an unknown – he does not understand its subject matter. This gives cause for concern in a world where so much of the high standard of living – readily taken for granted – is a function of technological and production achievement. The reason for this inability to understand is not necessarily lack of some specific knowledge, but lack of judgement about the sum total of scientific and technological development and an ignorance of where specific parts fit into its spectrum. The state of development and the consequent climate of discussion in these two broad fields of science is in considerable contrast, and this complicates the handling of and the approach to their respective contributions in a common production context.

Apart from the contributions of the natural, applied, or the social sciences, those responsible for manufacture will be concerned with a number of techniques. These are frequently associated with systems and procedures, and although derived and developed from scientific method, they are usually more linked with administrative skill and practice. In the field of cost accountancy, for instance, one normally talks about 'good practice'. Good practice, typically, simplifies collection of data and highlights significant facts; characteristics which facilitate control. The following are, in essence, some of the techniques which are of interest to the production manager: standard costing, budgetary control, critical-path analysis, value analysis, line balancing, machine-shop loading. There are many more – some of greater, others of lesser substance. It is not always easy to define where one technique ends and another one starts; there can be overlap in their contents. Some techniques need considerable background and intellectual effort. Others are simple in structure and application. The introduction of computers to the field of production has stimulated the growth of new techniques, such as in the sphere of inventory control; it has also encouraged greater sophistication in already well-established fields – such as production planning. The application of these techniques, apart from knowing what they can achieve and how they work, requires judgement – it is, for example, an important economic decision when to go into great detail or when to take short cuts. Techniques tend to acquire specialists and advocates. These have to be evaluated, both initially and subsequently.

Finally, there are background subjects. This is the material that reflects the business environment, the background that provides judgement in policy development and decision-making. A quick selection from a broad spectrum could typically look as follows: The Law of Master and Servant, Patent Practice, Taxation, The Structure of Industry, Collective Bargaining, Development Areas, Restrictive Practices etc. None of these subjects, taken individually, are absolutely essential, but in summation they help to provide the well-rounded background of the man of affairs. In the past this aspect has been underestimated too often; in the field of production, as well as in commercial life, there is the need for such background, particularly at higher levels of authority. It is also important to bear in mind the speed with which this environment may change. The relationships between government and industry, on the single aspect of a national incomes policy, is a case in point.

It may be apparent from all the previous discussion that there is a great variety of subject matter from a number of different sources. They are not linked by educational or scientific argument, but by practical relevance and economic value. But such criteria may make for poor bedfellows. The disparity of approach, background, philosophy, and intellectual demand made by the various subject matter points to problems of training. There is the need for more than normal flexibility, compared with some other professions, and this makes considerable demands on students. It is unlikely that the same level of understanding and competence can be reached in all sections of such a wide spectrum of material. There may thus be the resultant temptation in an actual working situation to 'abdicate' in favour of the specialist.

4   THE STATE OF SUBJECT DEVELOPMENT

The study of production organization and management is essentially part of the wider field of management and business studies, although it is, of course, distinguished by the background aspects of its specific context. The setting within such broader framework is logical because, in practice, the production unit, too, is part of the larger organism – the business unit. Production is regarded by many as one of the three basic activities of a manufacturing business; the others being, respectively, the technical function, ie, the development of goods and/or services, and the sales function which offers and sells the goods and services to the outside world.

In an everyday working context one can also note the relationships between production and the other two basic activities or, alternatively, with such staff functions as personnel or purchasing. If these relationships did not exist the business would disintegrate.

Management studies, as a whole, have developed in scope in recent years, and this has been associated with a crystallization of major subject divisions; each suitable for specialist attention and represented by its own exponents. The rate of development of some of these subject divisions has been faster than with others. For instance, the study of personnel work or financial management seems more clearly defined and accepted. In one case the personnel department represents a more specialized function which can be seen as a whole by members of an organization. On the other hand, those concerned with financial administration and controls again generally reflect the common background of the accountancy profession, which provides suitable terms of reference. In contrast, the marketing and production functions seem to lack some of this cohesion. Practitioners in these functions, whether working in a line or staff capacity, may not find transfer, from industry to industry, quite so easy as, for instance, the accountant or the personnel manager. Of course, this may be partially explained by the importance of product, processing, or specific application knowledge. A contributory factor may be that such subjects as production are integrative themselves. To some observers, production reflects little more than a collection of specialisms or techniques, and the prominence of some of these constituent specialisms – such as work study or production control – seems to detract from the overall concept. Within business studies, the systems approach, which is gaining in acceptance, may, however, change the balance because of the greater stress put on interrelationships, which reflect the whole of a production system rather than the distinctiveness of a particular constituent.

Those integrative studies which consider the overall functions of the business make frequent reference to production matters as they affect the total company situation. Discussions about company strategy, business acquisition, product rationalization, investment proposals, diversification programmes, etc, frequently derive their strength from production arguments. In the manufacturing industries production absorbs a large share – sometimes an overwhelming part – of total business resources. Perhaps, with the exception of certain consumer goods (such as toiletries, which depend heavily on marketing expenditure), production needs, be they expressed in manpower, investment, or management resources, are such that they constitute a fundamental aspect of the total business operation.

The analytical techniques, which have developed in recent years and now form a considerable part of management studies, make extensive use of production material. Operational research is particularly prominent in this respect. For instance, linear-programming techniques are concerned with machine capacity optimization and work arrangement; queueing theory is interested in service facilities, such as raw material or tool stores, and how these could best handle random service needs. Similarly, operational research has made a contribution to quality control, maintenance systems, plant replacement scheduling, etc. In the same manner it is possible to refer to applied statistics, cybernetics, critical-path analysis, marginal costing, investment appraisal, managerial economics, etc. All these techniques use the production context for application and illustration, and may have contributed in this manner to the somewhat fragmented image of production studies.

Those management studies which concern themselves with organizational behaviour lean heavily on what are essentially production situations. Manager/subordinate relationships, particularly in a collective rather than an individual sense, suggest the shop floor. The foreman is associated with the factory, not with the office. Output and productivity are affected by tensions, disputes, frustrations, boredom, and group behaviour. All these are affected by work environment – monotony, limited control over the work task, dust, noise, dirt, etc, the physical and psychological setting of production. In turn, industrial relations and collective bargaining are largely concerned with the resultant attitudes of hourly-paid factory workers.

The training for production organization and management in the United Kingdom has developed along two distinct lines:

a **The generalist approach.** The approach here is to business studies as a whole, and production management is seen as a part of the total picture. Expressions of this approach can be seen at the London and Manchester Graduate Schools of Business Studies, the European Institute of Business Administration, Fontainebleau, France, and in the general professional studies encouraged and developed by the British Institute of Management.

b **The engineering approach.** Here the engineer in the manufacturing industries, irrespective of precise professional affiliations, has become increasingly concerned with the problems of manufacturing organization, because these influence the effectiveness of his contribution and the well-being of the business that provides his livelihood. The approach has an engineering or production flavour and is closely connected with technical education. It is associated with technical colleges, the new polytechnics, some of the technological universities and professional institutions, typically the Institution of Mechanical Engineers and the Institution of Production Engineers.

These two streams of training have different concepts, aims, and philosophies. From a national point of view there is room for both.

a THE GENERALIST APPROACH

The general approach of the business schools is full-time training at graduate level. Its appeal is to the younger man, under 30 years old. Fontainebleau, for instance, specifies that it will consider young men between 22 and 29 years. Previous practical business or industrial experience may be desirable but is not mandatory. Where a graduate has had prior industrial experience, his relative youthfulness may have limited his opportunities for work at senior level. The training concerned with the function of production is about 10 per cent of the total (the emphasis varies to some extent between establishments). This sounds modest, but production considerations and thinking permeate a good deal of the case material and the other subjects. It is appreciated that the graduates from this type of course, in view of their youthfulness and limited industrial experience, are unlikely to transfer immediately to a 'generalist' role when taking their next appointment – unless it be in a staff position, such as within a central management services or consulting department, or as a personal assistant to a senior executive. While movement upwards, after some years in an organization, might be accelerated, the graduate has in most cases to be prepared first for some work in a specialized field. How successful the transition from a business school into the field of industrial production will be in practice remains to be seen. The graduate business schools have not been established long enough in the United Kingdom for this to be adequately assessed. The climate and the environment of these two areas are, however, in sharp contrast; this could cause problems, particularly where the graduate has not had prior industrial experience. Such potential difficulties can and are somewhat anticipated by a programme of vacation or project work, which may form part of the course programme. (It is appreciated that such work has many other educational justifications – nevertheless, this aspect of familiarization, both ways, is worth specific mention.)

Apart from the graduate business schools and some of the other universities which are developing business studies, the 'generalist' approach is also developed by colleges of technology, particularly through the Higher National Diploma Course. The emphasis on production studies, as afforded by actual teaching resources, may vary somewhat, but the opportunities for close contact with local industries can be an advantage, especially with the development of sandwich courses, which by definition, require some of the training to be within industrial and commercial establishments. Along similar lines there is also the Diploma in Management Studies, sponsored jointly by the Department of Education and Science and the British Institute of Management (BIM). This course has been noteworthy in attracting students at evening classes. Most of these students work full-time in industry, are somewhat older and more mature, and can relate their studies more effectively to their work experience.

b THE ENGINEERING APPROACH

The engineering approach can best be appreciated by stating the views of one of the major Chartered Engineering Institutions. The Institution of Production Engineers, which in 1967 had over 15,000 members, defines the production engineer as follows:

'A Production Engineer is one who is competent by reason of education, training and experience in technology and management to determine the factors involved in the manufacture of commodities, and to direct the production processes to achieve the most efficient coordination of effort, with due consideration to quantity, quality and cost.'

This definition highlights the amalgam of the technology and organization of production. The choice of the examination subjects for the Membership Examination including, for example, Engineering Drawing, Chemistry, Control Engineering, Non-Metallic Materials, Tool Design, etc, reflects the wide spectrum of processes within the field of manufacturing. The organization of production is represented by the three subjects of the Fellowship Examination: Industrial Management; Management of Production; Management of Men.

This composite picture of technology and management can also be seen from the work of the Production Engineering Research Association of Great Britain (PERA). Established in 1947 and supported by industry, government, and professional institutions, it is primarily concerned with practical research to establish improved manufacturing methods and production techniques. Understandably, its work is largely concerned with engineering and metal-using processes, in relation to which it has issued many research reports. A more recent and significant development can be seen in the activities of its management economics department, which is interested in administrative and other problems not only in the field of production but relating also to some of the other business functions, such as personnel or finance.

Again, the Institution of Mechanical Engineers, a professional institution of long standing, with a total membership of 70,000, of which about 60 per cent are associated with the manufacturing industries, is also becoming increasingly concerned with matters of management and production organization. Management techniques now occupy a prominent place in its journal *The Chartered Mechanical Engineer*, and Part C of its Membership Examination is essentially related to aspects of industrial administration.

At the universities, production studies are available at graduate and undergraduate level within a technological context. The balance between the technological and administrative subjects varies somewhat between institutions, but one can detect a tendency for the administrative subjects to get more emphasis towards the later stages of a training course. Some of the technological subjects are taken to an advanced level at specialist centres, such as machine-tool technology at Manchester University. Apart from these, the full-time graduate courses that have developed most successfully – such as at Birmingham University or at Imperial College, London – are general in character, providing first the necessary background in an academic sense, and then permitting a student to specialize by means of a project or investigation. There is a tendency for such courses to be associated with operational research and quantitative methods of analysis, in which respect they resemble some aspects of the 'generalist' approach. At the undergraduate level the training at some of the new technological universities, such as at Brunel, Loughborough, and Aston, is linked, either partially or completely, with a sandwich form of training.

The work of the universities is paralleled by the colleges of technology, where growing opportunities exist for CNAA degrees (Council for National Academic Awards) and Higher National Certificate/Diploma Courses. There are stronger ties with the vocational aspects of workshop training, perhaps due to the context of technical studies in which most colleges operate. The organizational subject matter on such courses has been helped in those institutions which have also developed general business studies.

Overall, the growth of the subject development has had the benefit of the Industrial Training Act, 1964. It will be some years before the implications of this Act will be fully appreciated. Although the precise pattern of training may vary from industry to industry, as a function of the schemes put forward by the various industrial training boards, the training levies have nevertheless forced manufacturers to take a good look at their own training arrangements. Training officers, departments, and/or instruction schools have multiplied in recent years, and together with the sanctions of the levy these have had some influence on top-management attitudes to training. The training grants, which may offset the levy, are, of course, available for the usual craft training or apprenticeship, and they normally cover associated further education in the form of attendance at local technical colleges. Similar facilities may also be offered for corresponding commercial and clerical/administrative training. At a higher level there is financial support for supervisory and management training. This facilitates attendance on outside courses, conferences, etc, and further encourages training within a company under such auspices as the Training Within Industry Scheme (TWI). Grants may also be paid to those companies which provide off-the-job training at a separate company training centre. There are grants in respect of university and college students to cover their industrial work periods, as part of the sandwich form of training. If the Industrial Training Act succeeds in its purpose, it will provide an unprecedented opportunity for training in the field of production, its organization, and its range of technologies.

5 THE CHALLENGE TO PRODUCTION

Production, as a subject of inquiry and study, as a profession and career opportunity, may not have the most direct appeal to those about to start on their working life. There are varied reasons for this, and some of these reasons are deeply embedded in our social outlook and framework. The appeal of production, particularly at executive level, where talent has its opportunities, depends to some degree on the way a number of different challenges are met.

a Technological change

This is a major challenge. Unparalleled historically, both in the rate of change and its extent, it questions both existing technologies and the organizational systems associated with them. Often not only does the plant become obsolescent but the operator and the staff specialist as well. For instance, work study has more scope where manual operations are commonplace. When these operations become part of an automated machining centre, with feeds and speeds a function of machine design, then the scope for the work-study engineer contracts. Although it may be possible in the most general of terms to forecast broad technical developments, the future, with a specific process in a given firm, might well be unpredictable. There is nothing special about this, and the businessman approaches such risks as machine obsolescence in much the same way as risks in other directions. If he is cautious and knows his field he will be aware of the general trends in the related technologies. He is unlikely, however, to be familiar with the details of his competitors' product and process developments. Market opportunities – the life blood of business – may require the solution of technical and production problems before they can be fully taken.

The business requires resources to overcome these

challenges. Technical skill, versatility, and flexibility of outlook are important characteristics required by those responsible for the planning and execution of its production commitments. Such resourcefulness and resilience require a broad background, a readiness to discard techniques and processes when they are no longer economically viable, and a willingness to learn anew. This background is a function of the original training and its philosophy. The required attitudes may also stem from this source, but need to mature during the working life of the production manager or technologist. Precise packages of hard-learned facts are no longer as important as they were. Quick access to current and well-referenced information is more relevant. The ability to absorb and to apply new knowledge, irrespective of source, may well become the criterion in an ever-changing technological world. With the increasing rate of technological change, the tendency is to reduce the expected working life of a particular process or item of equipment. For instance, in the field of computer manufacture there have already been three 'generations' of computers in a span of less than twenty years. The change from thermionic valves to transistors, and now to micro-electronic circuitry, within computers has profoundly changed their capacity, construction, and manufacture. This continuous technological development has brought about unceasing economic change within the computer industry itself, as may be noted from the process of rationalization that has been going on over the last ten years.

It is interesting to compare such a rate of technical development with other periods of history. The Industrial Revolution, broadly within the period of 1760–1830 and which so profoundly affected the character of society and life within the United Kingdom, needed about a generation or more for each major technical change to work itself through an industry. The period 1500–1760 saw proportionately far fewer technical changes, and these on average took about fifty years, say two generations or, more significantly, nearly two average life spans, to make their impact.

Before 1500 the relevant time scale is in centuries! Comparing the past with the present, there is a tinge of effrontery in our pressure to persuade people to change and to adapt themselves continuously to new situations. After all, mankind in Europe and other comparative parts of the world has adapted itself already to the most unprecedented environmental changes in its history. Although not without its tensions and costs, the process of adaptation has been successful, and the reward, in material terms, has been the highest standard of living ever known by the bulk of the population. It is impossible to predict the ultimate outcome of this never-ending change. However, man has shown a remarkable resilience. When we stress the need for accepting change in the production situation we are addressing people who have become acquainted with and have found a certain amount of satisfaction from some of the rapid changes in modes of travel, entertainment, and general living patterns. Industrialized western man has become familiar with technical change, whether he likes it or not. The challenge in the United Kingdom is to turn more of this technical change to relative economic advantage. The challenge world wide is in social and moral terms.

b **The overemphasis of 'unique' experience**

The setting is the company with successful production and business performance. The profit record and return on capital are in line with, or even a little better than, the majority of companies in the given field or in related industries. The rate of business growth is beginning to decline and, while on the manufacturing side there may not be major criticism of physical operations, the tone and outlook is becoming increasingly conservative. If production methods have been associated with earlier energetic business development or were successfully evolved in response to some serious technical or production problems a few years ago, then they acquire the status of 'proven in our experience'. There is nothing wrong with such a concept; the analysis of production problems and processes reflects scientific method, which means regard for and the use of facts; and if the facts pointed to a particular solution five years ago and this made then all the difference in practice, then it would have been folly not to have acted correspondingly.

The risks occur with the ensuing state of mind; satisfaction with the particular solution to a specific or local production problem tempts the view that everything appertaining to a range of production methods could also be specific in context. As a result, many of the suggestions and stimuli which the outside world has to offer appear irrelevant. 'Very interesting, but in our trade this would not really work . . .' seems a commonplace reaction to outside stimulus. This view could be correct nine out of ten times; the tragedy is that the benefit of the tenth stimulus is lost when it would have been worthwhile to harness it. The process is cumulative, and a business which, in terms of success, is associated with a specific epoch or stage of development and is still preoccupied with this will gradually fall behind as such 'golden periods' recede progressively further into the past. Although certainly not confined to it, such developments can be seen typically in the smaller or medium-sized family business, controlled now perhaps by the third generation – a 'close company' for the purposes of taxation, with possible estate-duty problems. The relative decline can be rationalized on the state of trade, or the action of competitors, or government policy, etc. If it is due to the long-term disregard of much of the outside developments, then it is usually reflected by the limited or overspecialized experience of its technical and production personnel. The perception of technical and process opportunities, emanating possibly from other fields of knowledge, is limited or non-existent. The general attitude within the firm provides no clearing house for ideas as to how the company could tap the advances of technology in related fields. There is an inward-looking particularism which provides a basis for complacency – until the company and its processes fall so much behind that it either ceases trading or invites drastic re-organization by a new management. In substance, however unique or specialized a commercial and production setting may be at any given moment, its environment is dynamic, and this should ultimately be reflected in the company's management outlook.

c **The need for self-identification**

In ordinary conversation, when asking acquaintances about their professions (and when they happen to be accountants, solicitors, architects, etc) the reply is usually precise and definite: it comes in terms of professional affiliation and values. In contrast, until quite recently a similar question to someone in production, more often than not, might evoke a job description in a specific context. To give some indication of what the work was all about, the company, rather than the appointment, may then be described. Unless the man in question is fairly near the top, the organization is stressed, while the job attitude is defensive. Perhaps this reflects the company atmosphere and the subconscious 'organization man'! The pattern of such a state of mind can vary of course – despite some common undertones. A chartered mechanical engineer, in production, may well have a different outlook compared to the production man who started his working life on the shop floor of the company, but who has risen by his wits and intelligence to a senior production or management appointment. It could be argued, of course, that with the changes in our educational system over the last twenty years the latter case may become increasingly rare.

One can note that the practical, resourceful, but, in a scientific sense, untrained mind may be at increasing variance with the growing stream of 'trained intelligence' coming from our universities and technical colleges. The opportunities for staying at school which tempt the brighter child – presuming reasonable home environment – may well now attract some of those who, a generation earlier, would have started their working career at fourteen on 'the hard way up'. As success in production is not only a matter of trained intelligence but also a function of resourcefulness, character, attitude, and skill in human relations – attributes of a person to which educational institutions, especially at higher level, pay little formal attention – there may still be scope for the 'untrained' man in production, particularly if he has many assets in the latter category. In any case, there are now many external courses or training facilities available to companies for the specific development of their staff – if they regard this as desirable. The avenue is by no means closed, despite the broad changes in background.

In fact, it might be argued that there are dangers in what could be developed into a deterministic approach, such as: A is a graduate in, say, industrial engineering, therefore his career is along path X; B left school at fifteen and subsequently served a craft apprenticeship. His way is along path Y. While statistically this may well be so, if we look at a sufficiently large number of cases, there is a tendency to think too much in terms of such stratification. There is a wide spectrum of talents required for success in production, and perceptive opportunism is an important ingredient within the total range. Whether there is correlation between this factor and formal training has not been established. Success provides its own arguments, and if the success seems to have been achieved, either in the context of business or production, by the relative amateur, 'someone who dabbles in mechanics', then this would be a fact of life. Unfortunately this does not help self-identification or professional development in production. It tends to suggest that anyone, who has his wits about him, would do as well – which is nonsense.

Here, then, is the dilemma. On the one hand, we have the occasional 'outrageous' success of the amateur – and his success is well received in a sympathetic national climate. On the other side, there is professional stratification which is unlikely to form a complete catchment area of all the talents. Yet if there is no reasonable prospect of professional development, then production will have only limited appeal to the more ambitious minds. If the present situation continues, production and its related technological studies will continue to attract only a modest number of people, while the demand for social science subjects will increasingly absorb university facilities. The urge to do something 'with people', the view that human relations are paramount, deflects many from engineering and production studies. The tragedy is that in our factories there are some of the deepest human problems facing modern industrial society. Preparation in a functional and production context in many cases is the pathway to those positions where skill and understanding of human affairs becomes so important, and where the opportunity for betterment lies. The social scientist, unless he carries out responsible research work in industry, often finds his academic achievement irrelevant in the industrial world, and in those cases where he could have made an impact he may remain on the fringe, unless he has more to offer in a functional sense. The risk is that production – as so often has been the case in the past – is regarded as a residual occupation. If you cannot do anything more lucrative or cannot qualify for anything more respectable – then you may drift into production. However, real achievements need a better basis than such a social view.

Fortunately, long-term technical and industrial trends may help the standing of the technologist or the manager in production. The large firm and the large plant will tend to make proportionately larger contributions to the national output. Special emphasis may be given to such trends where large-scale operation goes together with modern manufacturing techniques. Many of the new processes of industrial significance made available by science in the last twenty-five years, such as in the fields of petrochemicals, drugs, man-made fibres, require heavy capital investment. The economic break-even point with such plant is often high, and this puts pressure on plant utilization and performance. A higher-quality engineer, chemist, or manager may be required. The necessary attributes for successful operation include more scientific resourcefulness, and this means being able to see and to utilize opportunities provided by scientific and technological developments in other fields. The flow of ideas and applications across industrial divisions is, of course, a well-known means for the general dissemination of new and improved techniques. The greater scale of operation gives more opportunities for the application of scientific methods. This may seem odd at first glance because, in principle, the use of such methods does not really depend on business size. However, where the marshalling of a multiplicity of facts and figures becomes an intellectual exercise there is the temptation to take short cuts or to apply 'rules of thumb'. Although smaller firms may have just as complex problems as the bigger ones, they usually have greater flexibility when a mistake is realized. But when the scale is large, the stakes high, the organization and production systems are gathering momentum, then the cost of risks and problems not rigorously assessed will become too high. The premium in the future will be more on those who, in a production context, can handle complex, large-scale problems.

Summing up the argument, there is then an opportunity for self-identification, given the continuation of the present broad trends in technology and industry. Self-identification is desirable, both from an individual and a social point of view, provided it is placed into a broad context and does not become the vehicle of professional particularism.

6 PROBLEMS OF SOCIAL AND ECONOMIC ENVIRONMENT

Most studies of production systems and organization concentrate, quite understandably, on the subject matter before them. They are concerned with what happens, typically, between 8 AM and 5 PM in the factory setting. After that we all go home. Perhaps this is as it should be; if the contribution by a writer in a production subject makes work smoother and production more efficient, then his object is achieved. Unfortunately perhaps for the tidiness of our approach, there are all sorts of intrusions into the context of production, which stem from the fact that our lives do not cease when we go home at 5 PM. (How many feel that

life only really starts when we are on our way home?)
Workers and executives lose their organizational roles, they
become citizens, electors, consumers. And next morning, as
the behavioural scientist and the observant manager will
acknowledge, they import some of their values, opinions,
and experiences back into their work situation.

There must be a limit to the width of any study if it is
going to have substance in the chosen field. In production,
then, the restriction is to the work, firm, or industry situation. The important point, however, is that we should be
explicitly aware that we have confined ourselves to a specified range of analysis; that the broader setting has some
bearing on production. For instance, the Factories Acts are
not just pieces of impersonal legislation, they reflect a social
purpose and philosophy. If we divorce our investigations
from their broad social context we do so because of convenience of analysis, not because the facts demand it.

a **Social values and production**

The discussion on the need for self-identification already
pointed to some social views which affect the standing of
production. The standing is not particularly high and, considering that the United Kingdom is regarded as one of the
advanced industrial nations, this may be regrettable. Our
social outlook does not seem to take much note of our
industrial and economic position. As 'a nation of shop-
keepers', commercial opportunities, 'city' opportunities,
have always attracted more than a disproportionate share
of enterprising talent. The field of production was seldom
viewed as a pathway to power and possession. It did not
reflect social success, and seemed physically and psycho-
logically unattractive. Compared to the older professions,
such as Law or Medicine, the civil service or an academic
career, its environment was chilling. Relative salary or
income projections, between production and such alternative opportunities, did little to compensate for a more
rigorous work setting and job discipline. The possibility of
self-employment, as in the professions, or the relative leisure
of an academic life, did not exist to any comparative extent.

Despite the modest size of the country and the range of its industries, there are many areas which are, geographically and socially, divorced from the industrial environment. The 'county' setting, the 'other England', although owing its prosperity to the large industrial markets near its doorsteps, does not look to industry or production, as such, for social or career satisfaction. This attitude is associated with a pattern of education – typically with the public school or the old foundation county-town type of grammar school – which is largely ignorant of and perhaps even prefers to ignore the activities of the industrial sector and the manner of life within it. Its teachers reflect a pattern of outlook and conformity that tends to be self-perpetuating. To many of their pupils industry will become another 'black box' world.

b The impact of marketing

The market place has always had some sort of fascination. As the livelihood of any production unit ultimately depends on it, it is natural that due regard is paid to it. The market place for industrial and capital goods tends, on the whole, to be discreet. The man in the street is not the customer, therefore little direct appeal is made to him. With consumer goods it is different. The calculated approach, usually based on the skilled analysis of customer psychology, is often blatant and overwhelming. The goods are presented in such a manner that makes many forget that they originally came off a production line – unless a defect or functional shortcoming has to be explained.

Production techniques and organization in some of the consumer-goods industries, such as toiletries, have now become so refined and skilled that they no longer form the major problems or cost areas. Distribution and marketing claim here the greater part of company resources or management attention. Where the setting is highly competitive, where there is industrial overcapacity, where product launching is an expensive risk, then the marketing function is emphasized. In such situations it may well make the difference between business success and pedestrian survival.

The tendency of the advertising and sales approach is to

play down production. The customer is explicitly or unconsciously invited to presume that he can take production for granted – unless there are some delivery problems, which just cannot be ignored, in which case the salesman 'apologizes' for his production people. But the customer doesn't wish to hear particularly about the problems and heartaches associated with his supplier's production. The experienced salesman knows that persuasion rests on the identification of the article with the potential user; the need development within the customer matters. Except for limited and specific cases, talking about your own production – assuming some competence here in the first place – does not help the sale. Within the market-orientated or even the production-orientated business, production as such has tended to remain anonymous to the outside world. In the eyes of its management, it either lacked the glamour or there seemed little incentive to glamorize it. Disregarding the technical and trade Press and its minority readership, it is only in recent years that attempts have been made to publicize production either in the context of company 'prestige' advertising or recruitment campaigns. It is a fact that there are fascinating production methods and processes; that the solution of production problems at the frontier of technical knowledge, both in the consumer and capital goods industries, can be an exciting and satisfying experience. But the economic return of publicity on such lines is difficult to measure – in the meantime we must earn our living, our goods must sell, the marketing people carry on.

c **Long-term structural changes**

A whole series of secular changes can be listed here which are gradually changing the production environment. The more significant are perhaps the following:

i   The long-term decline in the proportion of direct labour employed on production and the corresponding growth of indirect labour and functional staff.
ii   The gradual shortening of the basic working week.
iii The greater use of shift work in some industries.
iv   The risk of structural and technological unemployment.

v The relative growth of the service industries compared with the manufacturing sector.

The change in the 'labour mix' between direct and indirect labour varies from industry to industry, and its rate, in turn, is a function of technological change[3]. In some industries, such as the chemical industry and oil refining, direct production labour constitutes only a modest share of the total manpower. In the light engineering field, however, the emphasis has been the other way round, and it is here where the changes in some sections will become significant.

The challenges which such trends pose to the manager of production will increasingly be those of productivity measurement and achievement. There are also problems of motivation, incentive schemes, and work flexibility.

The institution of a shorter working week has been a long-term social aim of the trade-union movement, and its success is reflected in the progressive reduction of the formal working hours as illustrated by the following figures:

BASIC WORKING WEEK – MANUAL WORKERS

Year	Index No	Hours
1956	100	44·6
1958	99·7	
1960	98·0	
1962	95·1	
1964	94·6	
1966	91·1	
1968 (March)	90·7	40·4

Source: *Ministry of Labour Gazette*, April 1968

The data shows the trend towards the basic 40-hour week in the manufacturing industries.

It will be noted that the formal reduction in the total weekly working hours, as shown, has not been reflected in the reduction of the *actual* hours worked. For instance, the average, weekly hours actually worked by men in the manufacturing industries were 47·4 in 1960 and 45·6 in 1968

(April). Systematic overtime, to 'make the money up', is strongly entrenched in some industries; suffice it to say here that this involves problems of cost control, supervision, and work effectiveness.

The trend towards an increasing number of workers employed on shifts, either on a two-shift basis – a day and a night shift – or on three- and four-shift systems, is demonstrated by the following figures taken from a Ministry of Labour study of shift working in the manufacturing and allied industries:

	Manual workers covered by study	*Manual workers on shifts*	*% on shifts*
1954	5,493,000	667,500	12
1964	5,596,000	1,020,000	18

Ministry of Labour Gazette, April 1965

There are several distinct reasons for this trend. An important economic one is the ever-increasing cost of capital equipment which largely reflects its growing complexity and sophistication. The tendency towards shorter working hours reduces plant utilization and makes recovery of the initial outlay correspondingly more difficult. Such a situation could either slow down the rate of industrial investment – other things equal – or it could encourage the trend towards fuller plant utilization by double- or multi-shift systems, even if the actual shift-working time was relatively short. It may also be useful to reflect on the contribution of shift working in other countries to the relatively low cost of some of their manufactured exports. Admittedly, lower hourly labour rates are an important factor here, but these are gradually rising in some of the economically fast-developing countries, such as Japan. The willingness, however, to operate major industries, particularly those with heavy capital inputs, on a shift basis may become increasingly important in an internationally competitive setting.

The influence of technology can also be seen here. Firstly, in an economic sense, technical change, where it brings obsolescence, reduces the economic equipment's working life and tends to suggest more intensive utilization, while the plant is still up to date. Secondly, a plant may have to be on shift operation because its output is wanted at a specific time; typically, a power station. Opportunities for the storage of output are either non-existent or severely limited. Thirdly, many processes, particularly in the chemical industries, are so complex to start up, to operate safely, and to shut down that it would be uneconomic to relate production to conventional daytime working hours. Shift work has always been accepted in some industries because technically there never was much choice about it. Its spread to other industries, where the technical need may be less apparent and the economic argument meets indifference or evokes social resistance – it is in those industries where the challenge will come.

The structural changes in the overall pattern of employment are also of relevance. The industrial economist is familiar with the decline of some of the old-established industries, such as shipbuilding, coal-mining, cotton, etc, which may have a disproportionate regional impact on employment. The impact is seen not only in terms of local purchasing power but also in local job attitudes and labour relations. Despite government encouragement of industrial expansion in the development areas, relative unemployment figures remain high. For instance, in 1967 the seasonally adjusted percentage of wholly unemployed to total employees was as follows:

Great Britain	2·2
London and South-Eastern Region	1·6
Northern Region	3·8
Scottish Region	3·7

Source: *Ministry of Labour Gazette*

Although quite telling, these overall figures do not necessarily do justice to local areas of particular difficulty.

Long periods of unemployment may engender a defensive climate of social opinion which could resist change and development and in this manner create a vicious circle.

Technological unemployment so far has not had the attention given to structural unemployment, perhaps because it has no strong geographical pattern and is therefore not regarded as a social problem of the same magnitude. Relatively full employment, outside the development areas, has also masked its impact, but whether this will continue, remains an open question. With continuing technical change and a possible acceleration of its rate, problems of retraining workers, staff, and managers who may become obsolescent will be increasingly important. With senior staff changing to another career, perhaps in middle age, there may be special difficulties. The risk that some workers may become unemployable may also have to be faced.

Finally, there is the long-term trend towards the growth of service industries which, in terms of employment and capital invested, may make the manufacturing sector less dominant within the national economy. This trend towards a 'mature national economy', with steps leading from an initially agrarian economy to industrial development and then to growing service industries, is a phenomenon observed in several advanced industrial countries. Such a development may continue further in the United Kingdom, perhaps on similar lines to the United States. The basis for such developments is perhaps illustrated by the fact that all of us can eat and drink only so much per day and that, for the moment at least, we can drive only one car at a time. Our growth of consumption of physical goods may be slowing down because of our physical limitations as human beings, and our future standards of living may be increasingly associated with the provision of services as, for instance, travel and entertainment.

Summing up the underlying meaning of long-term structural trends, the production environment is continu-

PERCENTAGE COMPOSITION OF TOTAL EMPLOYMENT
BETWEEN PRIMARY, SECONDARY, AND TERTIARY
OCCUPATIONS (1962–3 AVERAGE)

Country	Primary (agriculture, mining)	Secondary (manufacturing, construction, etc)	Tertiary (services, transport, distribution, etc)
Japan	30·0	30·3	39·7
Italy	27·8	39·4	32·8
France	21·1	37·0	41·9
West Germany	14·3	42·6	39·5
USA	8·9	30·7	60·4
UK	6·7	44·0	49·3

Source: OECD Manpower Statistics

ously changing – we have a dynamic setting. In some respects the changes may be almost imperceptible; in other cases the reminder is quite explicit, such as with the closing down of a shipyard or a factory. Our views about production must take change into account, even if our forward horizon may be limited at times.

d **The educational challenge**

The challenge of education is on a broader front than just production, but it is on the manufacturing side of industry that the challenge is most acutely felt. We now have the most expensive and developed system of education in our history. The long-term trends are towards a higher school-leaving age. University education has rapidly expanded and in 1967 about 185,000 full-time students attended forty-four universities. The methods and philosophy of education are also changing, and there is growing emphasis on individual self-development and expression. Irrespective of the individual career choice of a student, the physical number of trained minds, ready to make a contribution, available to industry and production, will increase. (This is a function of total numbers, not that production is necessarily able to attract a relatively larger share of talent.)

The challenge is the proper utilization of the human resources made available. The use of human capabilities, if expressed on a similar percentage basis as, for instance, machine-tool utilization, would look appalling. Never mind the 'high flyer', the 'rising young executive' – this protégé of management seminars – it is the bulk of humanity, now more educated, but often proportionately less used, that is the problem. As far as the businessman is concerned, labour is a 'production input' which he buys to specification – not necessarily entirely his specification, but a specification nevertheless. If the performance is to requirements, even allowing for the imperfections of the labour market in the economic sense, then one of his basic objects is achieved. With all his other business preoccupations, he may well excuse himself from inquiring too much into the problems of the suppliers of such labour who see that most of their human potentialities will be wasted.

It is general human experience that many a facility learned, but unused, tends to wither, and in that sense wastage may be greatest in the early years of a working life. The phenomenon may be observed in many walks of life, but it is in production where the contrast between the available potential and the actual work requirements is so often at its starkest. We have a basic social problem. Education points in one direction, the development of individual capacity and self-expression, and industry, which apart from a specialist and management minority, requires the bulk of its workpeople to accept the discipline of organization and a conformity in behaviour, points, in a sense, the other way. The implicit discouragement of self-expression, which forms part of many work situations, has its carry-over into social and public life. To what extent can apathy, indifference, cynicism – the products of non-participation – be left behind, when we leave our work situation? Industrial realities are incongruous with some of our concepts of a democratic society. The resolution of the dilemma may require the highest order of industrial and political leadership. Those in production are faced with the expressions and tensions of the contrast. An awareness of the deeper roots of the problem will help in the development of more satisfying relationships in the work situation.

REFERENCES

1 T. Lupton: *Management and the Social Sciences*, Hutchinson, 1966.
2 W. Brown: *Exploration in Management*, Heinemann, 1960.
3 *Ministry of Labour Gazette*, July 1967: 'The Occupational Effects of Technological Change'.

FURTHER READING

H. L. Timms: *The Production Function in Business*, R. D. Irwin Inc, 1966.

CHAPTER TWO

The New Product

1 PRODUCT POLICIES

In the long run a business needs to have a purpose. For a while it may exist without one – at least without one that is explicitly defined. If it exists; if it has customers and is a profitable venture, this may suffice for the time being. But the business will have to face the problems set by a changing environment, and then decisions will be called for as to the general course of action it should follow. An expression of purpose will provide a focus. It will embrace a set of related objectives which will constitute the pivot of company philosophy and thinking. However, to say that a company's purpose is to make money is to express a platitude which, on closer investigation, is not always even true. A statement of this kind, as P. Drucker[1] states so forcefully, is inadequate as a guide to those responsible, within a company, for the development of plans and policies. The purpose of a business is better conceived in terms of the provision of a specific range of goods and services, to satisfy an expressed or potential demand. If such a purpose is soundly perceived and the company is reasonably effective in its business operations, then profits ought to follow anyway.

The nature of product policies and their relevance to production may perhaps be better understood if the following terms are defined first:

BUSINESS PURPOSE

This is a statement of intent which describes the role of the business in relation to the outside world. In an economic sense this is expressed in terms of the goods and services offered, to meet a known or expected demand.

BUSINESS OBJECTIVES

These are component aims which give practical expression to the statement of intent.

STRATEGY

This is the disposition and arrangement of resources to achieve business objectives in a competitive market setting.

The development of overall business objectives gives expression to policies which provide the terms of reference for planning, execution, and control. Urwick's definition[2], given below, conveys most comprehensively the meaning of the term.

POLICY

This expresses the broad outline of the course it is hoped to pursue and which will govern the detailed action of all who work to the policy. The policy then becomes the governing theory and reappears in a modified form at each level of authority and for each technical function.

Taking a hypothetical example of a firm of crane manufacturers, it would be possible to express the various steps in the development of product policies as follows:

BUSINESS PURPOSE

We exist to solve load-lifting problems.

BUSINESS OBJECTIVES

1　We intend to manufacture overhead travelling cranes, specially suited for the iron and steel industries.
2　We intend to become the market leaders and to have a dominant share in the business for overhead cranes, with a lifting capacity in excess of fifty tons, etc.

STRATEGY

1　We intend to work closely with other steelworks equipment manufacturers and are prepared to join consortia for large-scale contracts, wherever necessary.
2　We associate ourselves closely with the steelworks design teams, so that our proposed installation is integrated within the overall plant design concept at the formative stage, etc.

PRODUCT POLICIES

1 There shall be continuous development of our basic crane designs, to correspond with changes in steelmaking practice.

2 It shall be possible to operate all our equipment either locally or remotely, etc.

It may be noted that the distinction between strategy and product policies could be rather fine. In this context, strategy reflects an emphasis on given market or business situations while product policies suggest a general setting and a longer time scale.

a **Market aspects**

The development of product policies involves an appraisal of the particular market situation within which a company finds itself. The picture of a heavy electrical equipment manufacturer, with the Central Electricity Generating Board as a monopoly buyer in the home market, is quite different from that of a 'convenience' food business about to launch a new breakfast cereal. In one case the customer is economically powerful and technically sophisticated and encourages his suppliers to develop bigger and more complex generating plant. In the other there is a mass market, without technical views, but which may require a brand image and all the art of marketing for volume acceptance. There is no doubt that two such very contrasting situations require different product policies, and this has repercussions affecting production. From the marketing point of view there seems to be little in common, as far as the two companies are concerned.

On reflection there is much they have in common. Both seek opportunities in their respective markets, and their success depends on the skill of their management in exploiting the opportunities offered to them. The market opportunities exist in or are hinted at by the outside world, and apart from their perception, much depends on the disposition of company resources so as to achieve the greatest possible results. As opportunities in a competitive world will be on a time scale, the speed at which they can be utilized is important. It is therefore not only a matter of the scale of a company's resources, put to a given product opportunity, but also one of speed at which such resources can be switched to the desired goal. In both the examples given, one can visualize the repercussions on production when market opportunities are seen and taken. An element of flexibility is required which does not necessarily ease the life of those responsible for production. Nevertheless, it is the global business opportunity which matters, despite the seeming dislocation which commercial opportunism may bring about in some specific sectors of the enterprise.

b **Resource utilization**

Despite the size and strength of some of the modern business corporations, the resources available to a firm are limited, and the skill in resource utilization is in their disposition to maximum advantage. The resources of a company can be grouped broadly into two general categories. Firstly, we have those which are reflected in its balance sheet, such as cash, investments, fixed and current assets. The other category reflects essentially human capabilities and, as such, is not financially valued, except perhaps indirectly by a company's profit record. Under such a heading could be put 'know-how', experience, managerial resources, technological strength, etc. Concentrating on those resources, which are particularly relevant to the production context, we have, typically, the following:

i   *Production capacity.*   This is the physical expression of the manufacturing floor space available and the nature of the installed equipment.

ii *Labour availability.*   This is more than mere numbers and presumes the skills required for the operation of the appropriate manufacturing equipment.

iii *Technological capacity.*   This relates to the company's strength in research, development, and production/process engineering.

iv *Managerial resources.*   This summarizes the trained and motivated intelligence, applied to the direction, planning, and execution of manufacturing activities.

Production capacity.   The expression of available manufacturing floor space covers not only the physical areas in which production takes place but also such associated sections as inspection and control areas, warehouses, component and raw material stores. In some industries, such as with the manufacture of glass or plastic containers, the storage areas may well exceed the actual production floor space.

The assessment of floor-space availability starts with the appraisal of vacant or under-used areas. A given building frame may not precisely match momentary production requirements, and unused areas invite 'temporary use', which makes these areas 'indispensable', in due course, to those manufacturing departments which have spread into them. Where such unused or under-used areas do not exist, the possibility of expansion, either within the building or site context, may be relevant. Such a growth in facilities has, of course, a time and a cost aspect, which must form part of a total appraisal. The type of building, such as its suitability for precision or quality work, a smooth work flow and its provision of important works services, such as steam, electric power, compressed air, etc, can be quite critical in some cases. A mere enumeration of area is insufficient; the manufacturing purpose must be satisfied.

Again, the existing resources, represented by the installed equipment, require careful scrutiny. For instance, with general-purpose machine tools, a good deal of flexibility is possible in terms of engineering or size specification. A plant, first conceived for a general or even a specific purpose, may have quite a surprising technical versatility. That does not mean that it is competitive economically for every conceivable operation that could be obtained from it. If a given plant concept reflects the product mix to date, a new product may well question its suitability in the new context. There might well be the temptation to think too much in terms of improvisation, using existing equipment as a point of departure. Such a 'low-cost route' into a new manufacturing situation, even if a related one, has its long-term risks. If product development and manufacture is too much conditioned, at the formative thinking stage, by the physical proximity of existing production plant, then alternative manufacturing routes, which could ultimately be superior, might be dismissed without sufficient consideration. Existing physical resources must not precondition basic thinking.

Two other aspects are relevant to a consideration of production capacity. One is concerned with plant utilization, where there is scope for multi-shift working. Some of its problems will be discussed subsequently. The other deals with the subcontracting of work, ie, the utilization of other available resources, which are not, however, subject to the detailed organizational control of the firm. How much is made within or bought from outside the company is a matter of economics and, possibly, strategy. It certainly is a matter of production capacity, but brings in also the consideration of other company resources. Where the work load is rather variable and where a business situation permits it, the use of subcontractors is often widespread, particularly where a range of specialist engineering or assembly tasks is required on a unit or small batch production basis.

Labour availability. While the machine may have replaced the manual worker in a number of automated processes, operating and craft skills remain an important industrial need. The availability of suitable labour may be an important manufacturing consideration, particularly where the new product extends the range of production commitments. Where the economics or the technology of a production process requires a shift-work system, such a need for labour may become acute, and even if labour can be secured, the costs involved, either in the form of inducement benefits or the acceptance of lower productivity rates, could be considerable. Again, if a wide range or a high standard of skills is called for the problems are correspondingly increased, especially in areas of full employment. In those industries where production processes are fully understood in scientific terms and where the art and discretion of an operator can be entirely eliminated it is possible to 'deskill' work, so that with careful technological control a relatively unskilled man (or woman) can take the place of a skilled operator. However, despite all training manuals and operator-training schemes, a new product, if untried on the scale envisaged, will not make it easy to forecast all the skills that may be needed for every operation. There is an element of risk about such operations, and until these can be defined in detail, when the new plant has been proved – and this is quite important – the labour estimates will remain provisional.

It is a fact of life that by history or tradition certain craft skills have a geographical concentration. It may be possible to move key workers from one part of the country to another, but the exercise becomes expensive where large numbers are involved. The writer recalls many an early morning train journey from London to Luton with the director of a hat-making business. This gentleman had repeatedly considered moving his plant from Luton to London, where his main fashion market was. There was, however, no prospect in London of getting sufficient labour of suitable skill and experience. In Luton, with its tradition of hat-making, such labour was available. The business stayed in Luton.

The impact of the Industrial Training Act 1964 may, in due course, change the situation as far as the training of suitable labour is concerned. The cost of training workpeople in a district where the right type of skill and experience was not hitherto available can be set in part or as a whole against the industrial training levy for the industry concerned. Nevertheless, the time and managerial resources needed to achieve the desired production performance levels may remain an important consideration.

Technological capacity. There is the general tendency for new companies and products to follow technological developments, because such developments present commercial opportunities which were either not envisaged before or were impracticable with an earlier level of technological attainment. The continuous repercussions of technical change provide a setting where the company with suitable technological resources has more opportunities than the business without them, and while the perception of opportunities is not an automatic prescription for business success, it is likely to enhance its prospects. The resources to be considered are in the field of research, development, production, or process engineering. They reflect the aggregate of skilled and experienced professional manpower and are a function of actual numbers as well as organizational factors, which give the work of various individuals a functional effectiveness. The skill in controlling the operation and cost levels of technological resources is a special skill because the measurement of their effectiveness is complex and there is the continuous risk of misdirection, specially when the unknowns of a research situation have to be faced. Policy considerations, in respect of new products, have to take into account the spectrum and levels of existing technological resources, the possible procurement of additional resources and their general deployment. Technological resources are expensive, and the economics of their use have to be carefully considered. New product requirements are best expressed in terms of detailed technological resource specifications; otherwise there is the temptation, particularly with the non-technical administrator, to allocate resources in a manner which is administratively understandable but technically inappropriate. This may be particularly the case where the product is on the fringe of established knowledge or has composite problems which cut across normally accepted academic subject divisions. The range of specialist skills is important, as well as the calibre of the personnel involved. Where there are specialist problems, such as in the field of industrial finishes or corrosion protection, there may be few people with the appropriate experience, and if these are not available it might require one or two years before even a modicum of such experience may be accumulated.

Outside assistance, in the form of consultants, may be feasible, but such avenues may be limited by the specificness of a given situation. Of greater practical importance could be the acquisition of 'know-how' and manufacturing licences from companies, already in the product field, say in the

United States. Long-term arrangements to exchange technical information could lead to a division of labour in research and development, and therefore make more economic use of technological resources. Of course, much depends on the cost of such arrangements, which in turn reflects the bargaining strength of the company. Such strength is understandably influenced by the technological capacity of the company in the first place.

Managerial resources. Many an argument for the financial take-over of a company has been associated either with the wish to get hold of managerial resources in a specific field of business or to give opportunities to such existing resources in a field which offered promise upon suitable reorganization. Managerial resources have become part of the logistics of company strategy. It is a relevant factor in the development of new product policies, particularly where this is linked with company growth, both physically in terms of assets controlled and organizationally. The successful launching of new products in a competitive field requires managerial strength in the various functions of the business and at each appropriate level of authority. The requirements are increasingly expressed not only in functional skills but also in terms of professional management techniques. Successful application of these, in turn, presumes appropriate training, guided experience, and early responsibilities. The time scale of such developments is considerable.

Much depends on the character and the attitudes of line management. In production and marketing the stresses caused by a new product venture may be particularly noticeable at the middle levels of management, and, unless the organizational structure is strengthened at this level in anticipation of new product developments, a number of general difficulties can arise. In an extremity much of the management and staff resources may have to be thrown into a crisis situation, and this in turn can weaken a company in other fields of operation. Both the character and the attitudes of line management are influenced by the spirit and morale within the organization as a whole, and this in turn is a function of its leadership and overall direction. Motivation is important.

It is also necessary in this context to consider the calibre of the managerial resources available to the company. This includes intellectual ability, the personal skills required for the direct and effective control of subordinates, as well as the resourcefulness to deal with the unprecedented, arising from a novel situation. Cohesiveness also matters: a team of well-integrated executives is more effective than the sum total of individual contributions. Where the new product suggests an organization structure, within its field, that differs from that already established within the company, such cohesiveness may be at a particular premium.

Managerial resources can be bought, recruited, or developed within the firm. Long-term product policies may require corresponding management development plans. The resources need to be husbanded because they are scarce and expensive; how to get the most out of its managers is a challenge to company leadership. For the effective development of a new product the managerial resources must exist.

c Product life

The expected product life is an important consideration in the development of product policies. The factors which, in turn, influence its length are numerous and complex and reflect in some respects a dialogue between the company and its customers. There are many instances where a market, capricious and fashion conscious, puts a limit to the lifetime of a product, but the manufacturer's persuasiveness in advertising, branding, and imagery could influence such market behaviour. Then it becomes a matter of company resources and their general disposition, within the overall business strategy. In an economic sense some products may have an indefinite life because they satisfy basic and inherent human wants. But here, too, may be the risk of substitution if a basic need can one day be satisfied by a different product. From a marketing point of view a product may be delineated in a number of ways, by design, function, style; or, as in the case with chocolate, by packaging. If a particular product, so branded, then develops its own market its life and the time span during which it consumes resources and yields an income may be separated from the general strategy of the company. Branded products may come and go, each exploiting a possible market opportunity, yet despite the product brand permutation of the day, the company in fact manufactures broadly the same commodity.

From a company point of view the product life may be measured from its inception or launching date until its contribution in relation to employed assets falls below what the company regards as reasonable or could get by deploying its resources in other ways. Before the launching date the product is in an embryo or development stage; it consumes company resources against a promise of benefits to come. These benefits need, of course, to be evaluated against the resources thus committed, and such an exercise is similar in nature to investment appraisal; discounted cash flow techniques and other methods are available. Again the termination of a given product life needs careful consideration. It may be relatively easy to assess the benefits derived from the product. (In this context the term 'benefit' expresses the difference between product revenue and such direct costs and variable overheads, as can be clearly associated with the product, ie, the contribution it makes.) A decision on strict economic considerations may be relatively straightforward; the difficulties could be organizational. As Drucker[3] indicates, there is often a nostalgia for a product which was yesterday's success story, particularly if management reputation is associated with it. The organization may have had a hard and long history of perfecting the performance and manufacture of a given product. Now, streamlined and competent in this particular product field, it finds the trend of market developments against it. In such a case there is a strong temptation to apply organizational momentum to continue with a product, perhaps for longer than is economically justifiable. After all, there is always the hope of a favourable change in the market situation.

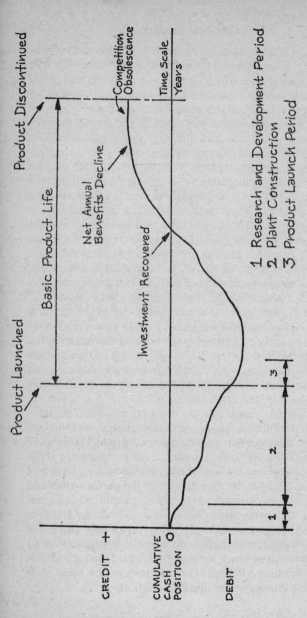

Fig. 2 PRODUCT LIFE IN TERMS OF CASH FLOW

NOTE: The Cash Flow is visualised on a *Discounted Cash Flow (DCF) basis* at the rate at which the company can secure long-term finance

1 Research and Development Period
2 Plant Construction
3 Product Launch Period

Product life in terms of resource use and benefit can be illustrated diagrammatically as in Fig. 2.

The opposite graph quantifies resource use and benefits achieved and shows, in cumulative terms, the net cash in- and outflow in respect of the product. The initial cash outflow reflects the preparatory work involved in product design, manufacturing process development, and plant investment. It can, of course, also include initial marketing expenditure, which, during the early phase of product launching, may well exceed the benefits from the initial sales volume attained. The resources required and the time necessary to bring a new product to the market are a function of the industry involved, plant flexibility, scale of operations, and many other factors. A new, mass-produced car, such as the Ford Cortina, took about $2\frac{1}{2}$ years to plan and required an investment of over £12 million. In this case the product was a variant of proved models, and although distinctive in style, it did not involve fundamental changes in technology. However, as Davies and McCarthy[4] illustrate, where the new product constitutes a major technical innovation, the initial product preparation period, up to the stage of net positive annual cash flow only, may well be up to ten years in such industries as the manufacture of aircraft and chemicals. It must also be remembered that the net positive cash flow starts from the minimum point on the cumulative cash flow curve and that it may still be many years in the future before the initial investment is recouped. With such a lengthening time scale, there is the correspondingly greater risk of loss, due to competition or obsolescence, when for a given annual sales volume a long product life is needed.

Where a company has a range of products – and this perhaps is the most frequent case – a specific product and its envisaged life must be related to the product group as a whole. The various products are competitive in resource use, and priorities need to be established. If the new product affects the sales of some of the company's established lines, rather than those of competitors, its success will correspondingly be qualified. It is the sum of all the product contributions that matters in the long run, not the individual contributions. The character of the new line, in terms of product appeal, market sector, functional application, familiarity, or standardization may reinforce or diminish the standing of the complete product group. For instance, the Ford Cortina model completed a range from the small popular car to the big family limousine and reinforced the marketing claim that whatever the motoring needs of the individual or the family, the Ford Motor Co could meet it.

It is important therefore to consider product life in context; not only in terms of external competition, as far as this can ever be forecast, but also in the light of all other company developments that could have an influence on it. Also relevant is the precise timing of a market entry with a new product. A detailed discussion of the strategy and timing of new product launching is beyond the scope of this book, but many of the factors already stated would have to be considered within the framework of a short-term rather than a long-term situation.

2 MANUFACTURING LOGISTICS

The term 'logistics', derived from naval and military terminology, is used here to describe the evaluation and marshalling of the company's manufacturing resources in relation to the proposed new product. The discussion here will concern itself with the size and the nature of such resources. The nature of the resources includes production methods and processes, and this may have an influence on product design in the first instance. Although clearly interlinked in practice with many other manufacturing aspects, for the convenience of analysis it will be dealt with separately in the next section.

Excluding the case where everything is bought or manufactured outside the company – when in fact the business ceases to be a manufacturing enterprise – discussion about manufacturing resources will form part of the product planning process. Admittedly, production at the prototype or pilot-plant stage may be confined to an engineering or development department, but if fullscale commercial operation is envisaged those responsible for the direction, organization, and technical aspects of production must join the discussions. The question which then arises is how those responsible for production contribute to the new product deliberations, and in what manner of organization can their contribution be most effectively developed. The contribution is naturally made within the organizational structure of the firm, and although this may vary in response to its social, economic, and technological environment, one can nevertheless discern a basic pattern of relationships. As already mentioned in Chapter One, the three basic activities of a manufacturing business will involve:

i   The development, in a technical sense, of some goods or services.

ii   The actual provision of these goods and services.

iii   The selling of the goods and services thus made available.

How these basic activities are integrated and how those responsible for production make their contribution, within such a pattern, can conveniently be indicated by the diagram on page 58.

Such a description, in terms of functions, reflects the broad day-to-day operations of a typical manufacturing business. If new products and their development are a regular feature of a company's operation its organization structure may well make explicit provision for such an activity. When, however, a new product is a relatively infrequent event an *ad hoc* organization may come into existence to cover the particular development. There is nothing wrong, in principle, with an *ad hoc* arrangement, but care is required that terms of reference are properly specified and that any sub-group thus formed is adequately integrated within the organization as a whole.

In the larger company, particularly where there is a group organization, a good deal of the initial discussion may emanate from a head office services department. Such a unit may or may not be linked with a management services

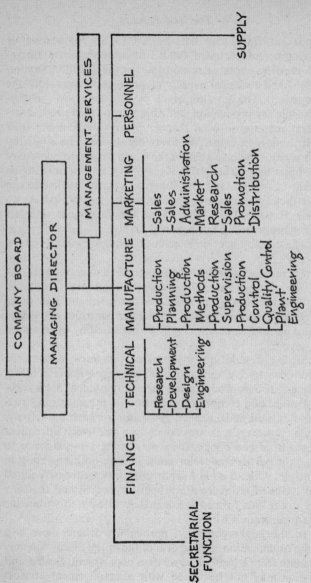

Fig. 3 THE BASIC ACTIVITIES OF A MANUFACTURING BUSINESS [TYPICAL ILLUSTRATION]

group. Where the company operates in a strong and fast-developing technological field, where long-term planning, technological forecasting, future resource projection, etc, are important, the contribution made by group members with manufacturing experience and background becomes particularly relevant. A head office services department concerned, either entirely or partially, with new products normally reports directly to the managing director of the company or to another board member concerned with forward planning. It may also have the guidance of a steering committee on matters of policy and direction, on which the manufacturing and technical/research functions may be represented at board or near board level. The department itself would include people drawn originally from manufacturing units, with either a broad background or, where required, specialist experience, such as in manufacturing processes. The department itself would have frequent working contact with the various operational groups. Where the scale of operation does not justify such an establishment, similar but simpler arrangements can be and are made. Most of the people involved would continue with their major tasks and functions, whether line or staff, but intermittently they 'change hats' and become involved with the planning of new products. Unfortunately, in practice, this 'changing of hats' in some cases is not an explicit exercise: companies drift into it. When discussions on non-routine matters are within the setting of day-to-day operations there is often a certain misalignment or, alternatively, an ineffectiveness about the proceedings. On the other hand, there could be a gain of flexibility from less formal relationships and closer association with current manufacturing activities. But whatever the precise situation or structure there is the need to:

1 Marshal and group together the right backgrounds of experience and skills – in our case, especially relating to matters of production. (Participation by the other main functions of the business is also assumed.)

2 Give such group guidance as to overall company policy as may from time to time be necessary.

3 Ensure the direct accountability of this group to a senior manager.

4 Properly integrate such group within the organization for functional effectiveness and overall contribution.

Contribution to product policy formulation. Policy-making – and here is meant effective policy-making, not just lip service – has become a complex task for the modern business corporation. Global views can, of course, still be formed without too much difficulty. But to make sure that such views are effective instruments of guidance rather than mere platitudes may now involve considerable study and staff work before the company's situation is accurately appreciated. A full-time or part-time working group, as already described, can make its contribution here. Basic manufacturing facilities can be related to sales expectations, both for the immediate future and the longer-term prospect. Such a matching operation will permit integration of two of the main business activities within the overall company context and help to harmonize marketing and production policies.

A basic contribution to policy-making will relate to the 'product mix' that a company wishes to develop to achieve its overall objects. Naturally, this has many other aspects besides production, but nevertheless the contribution to policy, from those responsible for manufacture, should be seen explicitly. The nature of the contribution can be visualized in terms of answers to the following questions:

a How wide a range of products shall we make?

b If we have a specific product, how many minor variations on this can we accept to satisfy specific, but perhaps infrequent, customers without upsetting the economics of our manufacturing processes?

c How much standardization shall we introduce in component manufacture and intermediate processes?

d How easily can we introduce new products without disrupting existing production?

The answer to these and many other comparative questions forms the structure of the policy-making contribution from the manufacturing side. This contribution then goes into the overall melting pot of general company policy-making. The point emphasized here is that there should be such a contribution to throw into the pot in the first place.

Contribution to long-term planning. Long-term planning is conceived here to cover the period from two to ten years in the future. Anything less than two years away may be too close to the present operating situation to be significant in the strategic sense. The future which is more than ten years distant may be too speculative to forecast. While much of the forecasting will concern environmental aspects, such as future market trends or the nature of social and political change, there is also an opportunity for technological forecasting related to the products and the manufacturing processes of tomorrow. A study of scientific literature and patent specifications will provide some indication of what might become available for commercial development and use some years hence. Also a company's own research and development work, if it is on a sufficiently substantial scale, may be projected forward and give a hint of future prospects. It will thus be feasible to visualize what might be the 'product mix' of the company in five to seven years' time. This, in turn, permits an appraisal of the scale and nature of the required manufacturing resources and the possible strategic location of new manufacturing plants.

Production feasibility analysis. Turning from the general contribution by production to overall company thinking, we come then to the particular evaluation of a specific new product. Most companies could make a given product – if time or money did not matter. Such an unrealistic situation is, of course, of little value in practice; we are primarily concerned with specific proposals in a given economic context. The appropriate question should be worded along the follow lines: 'Can you make x units of product A per month at a maximum unit cost of y? If you cannot, give basic reasons or, alternatively, specify your needs for making such a target feasible.' There are many permutations to such a dialogue, but whatever its precise nature, it should be an explicit exercise. It is here where the manufacturing departments make their most important contribution to company product planning.

The feasibility study covers a number of specific aspects, and the following are particularly important:

1 *General adequacy of available production capacity.* If the nature of the new product does not call for new or special equipment, then the assessment is the analysis of the existing factory work load. If an existing product is being run down, and the work capacity thus made available roughly matches the new capacity requirements the good fortune of such a coincidence may solve the problem. But in practice this may not often be the case. Investigation could then proceed in terms of more intensive plant utilization, such as overtime or shift-work arrangements. Alternatively, it could assess the installation of more equipment and such supporting facilities as may be required. Where the existing plant sections are utilized at different rates, an expansion appraisal will first concentrate on those plant items where the capacity limit has already been reached.

2 *The most appropriate method of manufacture.* This is developed in more detail in Chapter Three. The feasibility study for the manufacture of a new product concerns itself with the manner in which the product shall be made, particularly those parts of which the company has no working experience. There could be a number of ways in which the new article is made, and each route of manufacture may have its advantages and disadvantages in a technical and economic sense. An informed judgement has to establish, at this stage, that there is at least one way in which the product could be made that is technically sound and commercially viable.

3 *A critical review of existing production equipment and machines.* This appraisal relates the known characteristics and performance range of the installed production plant to the new product requirements. For instance, the new product may have a stringent assembly specification which, in turn, may require tighter machining tolerances

than existing equipment can achieve. The operative questions of the review are: 'Is all our equipment technically suitable? If not, what are the implications of the purchase and installation of more appropriate plant – assuming such plant exists? Alternatively, could some of our process requirements be contracted out?'

4 *The manning and work organization required for the new product.* These could vary in extent and nature from the company's present working pattern. New processes may require different utilization rates or cannot be conveniently stopped and restarted; a section may have to go on shifts while the rest of the plant stays on straight day work. Problems of supervision, manning, and pay differentials may follow. A new automated plant may require different skills, different operators, different managers, different maintenance facilities, etc. Such problems are not insurmountable, but they affect costs and therefore alter the economics of production.

5 *Production services needed for manufacture.* This covers all the 'utilities' that are required for production purposes, such as electric power, steam, water, compressed air, etc. It may be that some utilities are already used to full capacity, and while in most cases additional investments in extra capacity may resolve such limitations, there may be cases, such as with large-scale consumption of cooling water in some process industries, where the limitation is both physical and economic. Where the new product also requires a new kind of utility (such as refrigeration) or an existing service at a different specification (such as electric power at a higher voltage or steam at a higher pressure) special difficulties may arise; because if the incremental costs of such further services are solely ascribed to the new product they may well transform the economics of its manufacture.

6 *Space availability and layout concept.* While space may not necessarily be critical, if a new product requires the laying down of further production lines alongside existing manufacturing areas, which in turn have to continue

with existing production commitments, then an appraisal of floor-space requirements may become important. A production layout often requires storage and service areas which physically need more space than the actual production plant. A new and viable manufacturing section requires a clear and unimpeded work area for smooth production. The disposition of the earmarked production space may be as important as its extent.

The findings of such an analysis can provide a range of answers to the initial product-manufacturing inquiry. The spectrum of resources required and available for the new product can be stated in terms of equipment, manpower, etc. If the requirement cannot be met from existing resources the extent of the additional commitment can then be made explicit. Data can be provided as to the expected operating costs and the necessary amount of capital expenditure, if any. A number of suggestions can be submitted, where reductions in operating costs can be contrasted against increasing capital expenditures. The nature of risk in production can be indicated and, where possible, estimated.

The sum total of such an analysis may reject a new product proposition; alternatively, it could point to the complete contracting out of all manufacture. If this seems best in the light of the total company situation, then the manufacturing feasibility assessment has made its contribution to the general product-decision process. If the study supports the anticipated benefits of such a product venture it will set the stage for the detailed production planning.

It is in this manner that a decision to go ahead with the manufacture of a new product can have the benefit of an explicit investigation. Admittedly, the flow of information from and to those making the manufacturing evaluation is not confined to a specific brief and a consequent report. The product concept may still be crystallizing not only in a production but also, say, in a marketing sense. When thinking is formative a free interplay of thoughts and ideas is desirable – lest too much thinking goes along abortive lines. The marshalling of such a formative dialogue requires management skill, but if handled effectively it may achieve the desired results with great economy in staff time. A prompt feasibility evaluation of new products, expressed within the production context in plant, manpower, and pro-forma budgets, is important to a manufacturing enterprise.

3 PRODUCT DEVELOPMENT AND DESIGN

The embryo thoughts about a new product or design are usually expressed in terms of functional use, style, and market opportunities. This is appropriate – because if a new product concept fails on these counts there seems little point in taking the design further. But once such initial considerations justify the continuation of the design investigation, then manufacturing aspects have to be taken into account. It may well be that there is a range of initial design alternatives of corresponding appeal in style and function, and their consequent appraisal – in terms of manufacturing facilities – is an important step forward in the narrowing of the field of choice. One can usefully distinguish between those products where styling is an important design feature for the consumer market, such as with a radio set, and the functional/engineering design, say, for a bus engine. The designer, though not necessarily possessing special skills relating to production, must visualize how a product will be made, how its component parts fit together in assembly. He must have some idea of production processes and methods so that he can appreciate the role of those who have to evaluate his concept in terms of production and economics.

Materials

The choice of materials is an important first consideration. Quite apart from the intrinsic raw-material costs, the suitability of materials for specific production processes varies considerably. Much depends also on the scale of production: one may accept the problems of a specific production task in a special situation because the development of alternative methods or materials involves disproportionate costs in relation to the work in hand. But with mass production an investigation into alternative materials might be justified because of the multiplied benefit in terms of unit production times or costs. Some materials are worked with difficulty, resulting in higher reject rates or requiring a high degree of operator skill. Again, the varying rates at which materials can be cut affect the length of a work operation and, because of the time required, may influence labour costs. The casting and moulding properties of materials determine the complexity of the initial shapes produced and influence subsequent machining operations. Forming and joining processes permit alternative methods of construction which are a function of material properties. In substance, the choice of materials frequently determines the method of production, ie, the physical shaping of given objects. The finishing operations, whether with appearance or protection in mind, are again affected by the materials of construction.

Shapes

Where styling considerations are regarded of particular importance, there may be the temptation to put forward shapes and configurations which can be produced, but not necessarily at an acceptable cost. Shape may affect the choice of materials, particularly where structural strength has to be taken into account. It influences the raw material specification, the manner of production, the material-handling or flow requirements within the factory. In turn, assembly, layout, and tooling aspects may be involved. While such extensive repercussions may be comparatively rare, it is nevertheless important here that the designer and the production technologist are close to each other, so that opportunities for work simplification and economy are not overlooked. The consideration of shape may involve much detail, and where it is not critical from other aspects, the production technologist may well take the initiative on such points. For instance, rounding off corners or the precise location of holes can make a substantial difference to machining and assembly operations, in terms of speed of work and the deign of jigs (devices which clamp a component into position while it undergoes an operation).

Manufacturing facilities

The availability of suitable manufacturing equipment has already been considered in general terms when relating company resources to product policies. The context now is more specific and short term. The designer or development engineer has to relate his proposals to existing plant or proven equipment, which is the subject of a plant-investment project. One can also relate here such operating and maintenance skills as may be required to make the plant an effective working unit. In the extreme case manufacturing facilities without the requisite supporting skills may become liabilities rather than assets. It is therefore more appropriate to refer here to plant with its labour force rather than mere physical pieces of equipment.

Manufacturing facilities will affect the nature and sequence of production operations. They also affect the manner and speed of assembly. In terms of achievable precision, they can affect the whole functional purpose of the design. Detail variations in design have considerable influence on working speeds, reject rates, and, within a given quality specification, inspection costs. A good product design, both overall and in detail, has the working range of existing plant in mind. A close association with the production technologist is important. This does not mean that certain tasks or operations cannot be contracted out, but it is nevertheless important to make a clear evaluation as to what is involved and why this is necessary.

Technical and economic relationships

Disregarding, for the moment, the inflexibility of special-purpose equipment, the versatility of many general production units may be wider in a technical sense than what is practical in an economic context. This refers particularly to the temptation of producing a given part or shape because it can be done, but without looking at the costs involved. It is important in design to utilize the benefits of standardization. The final product 'image' may have a strong marketing

bias, but underneath that image it is standardization, interchangeability, group technology, simplification, etc, which
gives the cost and price advantage.

Standardization may be achieved by making most of the
components of a given product identical with those incorporated in the remainder of the company's product range.
This reduces the amount of stock that has to be carried in
finished items or raw materials and, by cutting down the diversity of work to be handled, it also simplifies manufacture
on the shop floor. The resulting longer batch runs give
further economies in machine operation. Standardization
can also be reflected in the use of nationally or internationally agreed standards (as developed by the British Standards
Institute or The International Standards Organization), for
instance, with simple fastening devices, nuts, screws, bolts,
etc. If these items are bought out the larger quantities, which
are a function of standardization, give better opportunities
for quantity discounts.

A product design which bears in mind the advantages of
group technology could again improve the economics of
manufacture. Group technology primarily makes use of the
family pattern of related parts, where for technical and functional reasons standardization cannot be complete. For instance, components, such as the shafts of electric motors,
can be identical except for one dimension, say, its length.
From a manufacturing point of view this need not affect the
raw material specification, such as the diameter of the steel
bar required for machining, or the setting up of a machine
tool. In an automated process only one of the control instructions needs to be altered. From this it can perhaps be
appreciated that group technology could reap a number of
the benefits of standardization yet allow a greater degree of
flexibility, which widens the span of its application.

Where competitive market pressures are strong and
where the unit costs of manufacture are heavily multiplied –
for better or for worse – by the quantities of mass production, then design is with precise cost limits in mind. If a
product cost target is set, as for instance, with a car, and

each component is given a cost ceiling, the ingenuity of design must be associated with an exhaustive knowledge of alternative production processes. The designer, production-technologist, and the cost accountant must work as one. Continuous, critical, questioning attitudes are essential, and the design analysis comes close to value analysis which is the critical appraisal of a product where its properties and construction, ie, its features and costs, are related to its functional role.

The design of a product will be to a cost. This in the first instance refers to the variable costs of manufacture; the use of materials and production hours. The functional and marketing aspects of a design must be associated with manufacturing effectiveness. Design, without regard to production, makes the new product vulnerable in a competitive world.

REFERENCES

1   P. Drucker: *The Practice of Management*, Pan Books, 1968.
2   L. F. Urwick: *The Elements of Administration*, Pitman, 1951.
3   P. Drucker: *Managing for Results*, Pan Books, 1968.
4   D. S. Davies, and M. C. McCarthy: *Introduction to Technological Economics*, Wiley, 1967.

FURTHER READING

T. L. Berg and A. Shuchman: *Product Strategy and Management*, Holt Rinehart and Winston Inc, 1963.
A. W. Willsmore: *Product Development and Design*, Pitman, 1950.
C. Hearn Buck: *Problems of Product Design and Development*, Pergamon, 1963.

CHAPTER THREE

The Planning of Production

It was found convenient, for the sake of analysis, to separate the policy and planning aspects related to a new product from the actual planning of its production. In practice, such a division looks rather artificial; production planning, as described in this chapter, is likely to start before all product aspects are resolved. The reasons for this are simple. Firstly, we have a feedback relationship between product planning and production planning: one affects the other. Secondly, where a company intends to launch a new product in a competitive setting, time could be 'of the essence'; it would be uneconomic to wait with one planning activity until the other had been completed in every respect. In most cases planning of production is partly sequential and partly parallel to the product deliberations.

The planning of production is an all-embracing concept. It includes the global considerations of planning production from a 'green field' site, where an open space is transformed into a working production unit. This is covered in sections 1 and 2 of this chapter. There is also the detail planning of every working operation in an established production section so that an operator, when given a new work task, can readily proceed with all the information to hand. This kind of production planning is described in section 3. There are, of course, many intermediate planning tasks which reflect particular manufacturing situations. As such they are an amalgam of the activities described in the various sections.

1 THE NEW PRODUCT – OVERALL PRODUCTION PLANNING

The starting point, for the manufacturing planning of a new product, is the decision by the company's management to go ahead with and to accept commitments in respect of the manufacture of this product. Such a decision is normally the result of prior evaluation and feasibility analysis, and some of the decision-making – subsequently associated with the planning phase – is in fact already implied in the assumptions that formed part of this initial decision process. It is presumed, in this context, that the following information is available to those responsible for the planning of production.

a A complete product specification, describing the construction, materials, functional performance, tolerances, quality, and test requirements, etc.

b Overall product design.

c Detail product or component drawings.

d Target date for the commencement of full production.

e Budget authorization, showing finance available for capital expenditure, tooling, work in progress, stocks, etc.

The work of planning may now proceed. With a project of any size the ramifications can be extensive, as may be visualized from the simplified task diagram, Fig. 4, which relates the various activities involved. The planning of a manufacturing programme requires the participation of many specialists, and good coordination of their activities is important. A project organization is required, and a project manager should be appointed. He will need clear terms of reference and, in turn, his accountability to top management for the progress and success of the project should be clearly defined.

Various task relationships can be developed, depending on the priorities of a given company situation. Assuming a given pattern of approach, the planning task can then be conveniently described in terms of groups of decisions. As planning involves continuous decision-making, such an approach is, in many ways, appropriate.

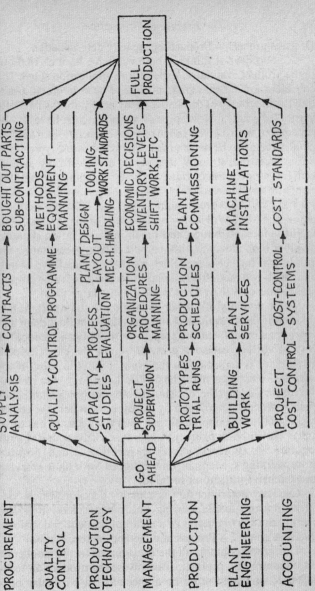

Fig. 4 SIMPLIFIED TASK DIAGRAM PRODUCTION PLANNING

Decision group 1 – Production capacity determination

A good deal of thinking here will have been carried out in the product evaluation/expenditure application stage. The considerations at that stage may have been in global terms only, with a range of capacities being acceptable as part of a feasibility study. Now precise requirements have to be stated, and with a given range of sales expectations a specific plant size has to be determined. There are cases, typically in the process industries, where plants are built only against firm forward contracts, but even here a risk and profitability evaluation will be necessary. Where there is no firm market, the risks will be correspondingly greater. How big shall the initial plant be? Will it stay under-used for many years, adding little in contribution and much in depreciation charges; or will it be inadequate within a year or two, necessitating the building of further plant? Such a situation may leave a company with two modest-sized plants, yielding the same output, at a higher cost than a competitor's one large plant.

The possibility of further expansion is an important factor, and if this is evaluated and considered in the design and layout of a manufacturing area it can simplify and reduce the cost of further capacity growth. Again the capacity of a given plant is very much a function of its utilization. If for technical reasons a plant has to be kept going for twenty-four hours a day the decision to operate on a multi-shift basis is already determined by the process. Where the choice is essentially in economic terms, then the decision has to be made explicitly. A plant that operates solely on a day shift requires an appreciably greater investment and possibly more working space than one designed with shift working and intensive utilization in mind.

Capacity determination is a major decision which concerns top and manufacturing line management. It is frequently the starting point of a chain of sequential decisions.

Decision group 2 – Process and methods determination

This group contains all the decisions as to the manner of manufacture of a product. It involves: the production technologist, who may often be a specialist in particular processes, for instance, in the heat treatment of steels; the industrial engineer, who is concerned generally with the analysis of working methods; and the cost accountant, who can evaluate alternative routes of manufacture in terms of labour or materials costs. As the choice of production methods is affected by the required rate of output, the links in analysis between groups 1 and 2 will be appreciated.

The decision processes in this group can be related to the development of *Outline Process Charts*. These charts describe in broad terms and in manufacturing sequence all the various operations that have to be carried out on a product and its constituents during the process of manufacture. They also specify the major inspection or quality control points within the chain of operations and indicate where materials enter and leave the process stream. A standard pattern of charts is now in common use, and the following symbols generally describe what happens during the process of manufacture.

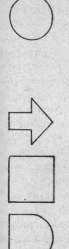

OPERATION. This describes the action that transforms the material in shape or in other properties. It includes assembly work or activities connected with the preparation of material for subsequent operation or transportation.

TRANSPORTATION. This describes the movement of an object from one location to another.

INSPECTION. This describes the activity of checking whether the object conforms with predetermined specifications.

DELAY. This indicates that an object is held up and cannot immediately proceed to the next operation.

STORAGE. This indicates that an object is deliberately kept at a certain place.

COMBINED ACTIVITY. This describes several actions carried out simultaneously. This particular symbol signifies that an operation and an inspection task are combined.

The sequence and nature of the manufacturing process can thus be shown in a clear manner, typically as in Fig. 5.

Such a chart serves as a guide to layout studies, material handling, and is the starting point for more detailed planning, method study, and work measurement.

Where a product can be manufactured in several alternative ways, the respective operating process charts may differ either on one particular, or several, or on all operations. The decision as to a particular operation, or a group of operations, such as, for instance, a casting as against a welding process, depends primarily on the following factors:

a The availability of actual operating equipment and its suitability for the proposed operations at the rate of output required.

b Relative capital costs, if the equipment still has to be purchased.

c Direct labour costs per unit of output.

d Materials costs per unit of output, with particular reference to the quality specification, if this affects the purchase price.

e The quality and reliability of the operations to be performed.

f The effect on previous or subsequent operations.

These are not the only factors, and the list could easily be extended when considering such aspects as power requirements, safety, nuisances, etc, but it may be noted already that the decision-making involves both technical and economic considerations.

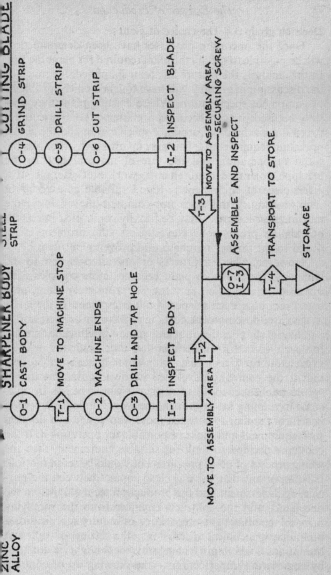

Fig. 5 SIMPLIFIED PROCESS CHART – MANUFACTURE OF PENCIL SHARPENER

Decision group 3 – The choice of plant

Once the operating processes have been determined, it will be possible to specify the plant required for manufacture. In this analysis the picture has been simplified, for much of the discussion in group 2 will have touched on the problems of equipment specification. Where existing plant may possibly be used, it then becomes a matter of comparison between the machine performance specification and the actual operating requirements. This may involve such aspects as the speed of operation and the rate of material feed to the machine, tolerance requirements, work unit size, etc. If a given piece of equipment is found suitable as a result of such an inquiry this does not complete the analysis; the machine, for instance, may be heavily committed in respect of existing production. Nevertheless, the problem is reduced to the further purchase of a proven plant item.

However, where a process or operation is new to the company, the choice of plant becomes more complex. The operation specification may suggest proprietary plant, or it could require special purpose-built equipment. If the latter is the case, development costs may have to be met, and if a potential supplier does not anticipate a worthwhile demand for such specialist equipment the user company will be expected to carry such costs. Nor would it necessarily follow that if the company developed its own equipment that it would be cheaper to do so or that it would be less troublesome in running in – although one would hope for a certain benefit of familiarity between those who design and develop such equipment and those responsible for operating it. If the company decided to look for suitable equipment, then the whole process of plant procurement would be set in motion. It is important that there is close contact between the purchasing department and the production technologist, on the one hand, and the contracts engineer from the supplying firm, on the other. The preparation of inquiry specifications, preliminary technical discussions, the sifting of different quotations – where price competitiveness might be qualified by engineering imperfections – the drawing up of contract specifications to define technical commitments in a commercial context, the detail changes, the late deliveries, the installation, and commissioning problems – all these are a function of plant choice. If the choice has been successful a plant comes into production at the specified time, with its output at the rate and inside the cost limits set. If, on the other hand, it has not been too fortunate, the alternative could be anything from inconvenience to disaster on all counts.

So far the application in mind has been for a specific operation in respect of a new product. If the proposed production programme makes only partial use of such equipment its possible application to other work, both existing and future, may be considered. The versatility of the proposed plant may be related to the projected technical developments within the company. There are also the related aspects of machine standardization and interchangeability, where this is feasible from a technical point of view. Furthermore, with the growing development of interlinked and automatic production units, the suitability of a new piece of equipment will have to be related to machine systems. It may no longer be economic to consider it in isolation, whatever its other merits may be.

Good decision-making in group 3 requires a sound and broad technical/production background, coupled with an understanding of economic principles as well as commercial realities.

Decision group 4 – Jig and tool design

Jig and tool design is a characteristic feature of the metal-working, engineering, and allied industries. Broadly speaking these industries use a wide range of standard machine tools. Such equipment is versatile in use, but it is not conceived for a particular manufacturing task. The actual work is carried out by a specially designed tool which is fixed to the machine and which achieves its purpose by using the power and motions the machine makes available to it. For instance, with a power press to shape car doors from flat sheets of steel the tool is, in essence, of the required car-door shape, and this is transcribed on to the sheet on impact. Similarly, a plastic injection-moulding machine is fitted with tools, so shaped internally that the hot material on flowing into the tool takes the required shape within the cavities provided. A jig, on the other hand, is a device which holds the work piece in position, so that the tool may carry out its operation. In this discussion jig and tool design is interpreted broadly, to include also such other fixtures – as distinct from machines – that may be required for the purpose of manufacturing operations.

The manufacture of jigs and tools is precision work which is either carried out in the tool room, a department specially set up for such a purpose, or contracted out to specialist suppliers. The designs and specifications are normally the responsibility of a drawing-office section within the production engineering department. High-precision work is costly because it requires greater care in operation, and it is usually slower as a result. It requires the 'tool-room skills' of time-served engineers whose hourly pay rates are high. Furthermore, the cost of quality control, either in inspection time or possible modification work, is considerable. It should be noted here that a tool is of little value in production until it has satisfactorily completed its production proving run and that the actual product, which could also have a high standard of precision, is in turn also to specification. The furnishing of tools for a particular manufacturing programme is often a substantial investment in its own right. For a car manufacturer to spend over £5 million on the tools to manufacture a new model is no longer exceptional. Similarly, a single press tool could constitute an investment in excess of £10,000. The economics of such investments require considerable attention, and this is a factor to consider when evaluating a manufacturing programme as a whole.

Tool sophistication and expenditure may well be justified if it helps to cut down production times, material use, and handling operations – provided, of course, that the volume of output can always take the initial outlay. In this field technical expertise is important, but it must be coupled with careful costing.

Decision group 5 – Plant layout

The layout of a production plant frequently provokes discussions at the planning stage which become quite out of proportion to the advantages claimed for different layout concepts and, for that matter, often quite out of proportion to the facts available. This arises because layout decisions can have multiple aspects, and it is perhaps a matter of opinion as to which factors should be given priority. The various layout considerations will be more fully developed in Chapter Six, and it is only intended here to review those aspects which are related to the overall production planning of a new product.

It is only when an operations process chart has been developed and when the production plant has been defined that one can effectively evaluate a physical plant arrangement. In the first place, such an exercise is necessary to obtain an overall area requirement in square feet (or square metres). Such a requirement is a gross figure; space around machines has to be allowed for attendance, for on-the-spot maintenance, for the feed and removal of materials, work in progress, services, etc. The gross areas required can easily be three or four times the net machine space occupied, without adding such areas as cloakrooms, stores, and other ancillary departments.

The next aspect of importance to consider is the flow of work in the course of production. Only those sections of the total production period during which work is done on the product itself have an economic value. Material that is idle on the shop floor or that is handled needlessly incurs costs and effort. The shortest, quickest route of production is the aim of the industrial engineer – that member of the production function who is particularly concerned with methods and cost reduction. A plant arrangement that follows the pattern of the operations process chart in sequence often provides the most attractive layout from this point of view.

Normally, discussions about the required floor space and

the flow line of production are very different for a new factory, yet to be built, compared to an existing plant. Unless the factory site has a particular problem, a proposed factory provides good flexibility for initial arrangement with few physical constraints affecting the work of the layout engineer. Yet, even there, the layout can be 'optimized' in so many respects, with so many eventualities catered for, that the floor space and building requirements get out of hand and begin to affect the attractiveness of an investment. Economic considerations on current and capital account must be evaluated. This is particularly important when relating the planned production to the proposed layout. How long are the proposed production runs? Do we have small batch, large batch, or mass production? How variable is the intended production stream? Can we commit ourselves to a fixed layout for a long period ahead, or is flexibility more important? Where a new product layout has to be fitted within the given space limits of an existing plant, ingenuity of arrangement is often required, and the layout may well have to be a compromise between the needs of the new unit and those of the existing production section. Of course, the situation becomes more complex when existing and new production facilities have to be integrated to sustain a combined or composite production flow.

The development of an integrated and feasible layout is a major decision task, and the physical concept of the production unit begins to crystallize only at this stage.

Decision group 6 – Quality control

Just as it is necessary to develop a specification for production processes and the corresponding plant, so there will be a need to determine inspection processes and equipment. Quality control reflects the functional specification, developed for the product, and the importance which the company attaches to consumer satisfaction. Aspects of quality control will be developed more fully in Chapter Five. Suffice it to say here, that within the overall production planning function, quality control is best woven into the manufacturing system so that it does not, as such, impede or unduly delay the progress of work, yet ensures that none of the set quality requirements are in any way compromised.

In most companies of any size the quality-control function is represented by a separate department. It will be the joint task of the production technologist and those responsible for quality control to plan and to integrate the quality-control system within production as a whole.

Decision group 7 – Manning and Organization

When the work is defined and the plant specified it will be possible, with the aid of work study, to analyse the manning requirements of a new plant. Where comparative plant already exists, either within or outside the company, considerable prior experience may already be available in a related form. No doubt most companies already develop tentative manning requirements at the project evaluation stage because if this is not done, then there would be no indication of prospective labour costs; and if these are likely to be a substantial component of operating expense, then the whole investment proposition may be unrealistic.

The industrial engineer will determine the total operator work load of a production process in terms of 'standard' time (see Chapter Eleven). This presumes a given rate of work and a method analysis which provides the best available working method. Such standard times may either be based on measured work, recorded on other but related tasks, or may be estimated. Where standard times are expressed in hours, a transcription to the required number of operators on, say, an eight-hour day is simple arithmetic. In practice, a company may find that an output, based on standard times and corresponding manning, is seldom achieved, and if in the light of its general manufacturing experience actual output related to standard output per day corresponds to an 'efficiency' of, say, 80 per cent it may be realistic to allow for this in manning – particularly if a definite output target has to be met and there is no evidence that the effectiveness of operation is likely to improve. On this basis, the number of operators in a new production unit can be determined and, where appropriate, shift-manning requirements may be established. Once the number of operators is given and related to the technical nature of the production processes, the pattern of supervision can also be more closely defined. Also, an important point here is that as the labour content of operations is evaluated and the corresponding tasks are grouped into work roles, job evaluation and labour grade assessment can proceed and determine the types of labour required and their wage rates within the company context.

Furthermore, it will now also be possible to relate the new unit to the existing factory procedures and control systems; and it may well be that these have to be modified to achieve the effective integration of the new production unit. Responsibility for decision-making in group 7 rests with the factory management, which will frequently have available to it the staff services of a work study, personnel, and, possibly, an organization and methods section.

Other decision areas

The seven decision groups already listed summarize the most important areas in which overall production planning will proceed. There are, however, a number of other areas that could be of importance in specific cases, and some of these deserve mention:

a The planning of working capital and the cash-flow requirements for the new production unit. This requires decisions as to inventory levels and work in progress.

b The development of a procurement plan. Where some production operations are contracted out and materials have to be specially purchased, such activities have to be integrated with the overall production plans.

c The commissioning of the new plant and the organization of test runs.

2 THE NEW FACTORY

The outcome of decision-making in the previous section should now permit the complete statement of requirements for a new factory or a manufacturing area within an existing plant. Let us presume that the company is no longer able to expand on the factory sites from which it operates at present, and that a new site has to be found. Once we know the planned rate of output, the proposed equipment, floor-space requirements, services, the number of workpeople and staff, planning which is not directly associated with production, but takes its main terms of reference from it – may now proceed and a full brief can be prepared for a new manu-facturing plant with all its related activities, such as offices, stores, transport system, etc. We should stress that, in practice, the development of such a concept does not wait until all production planning is complete, for there are few 'perfect' sites where constraints do not affect planning. In most cases production planning and site planning proceed in parallel, although there are instances where large com-panies, operating for technical or distribution reasons with many small manufacturing units, have developed standard production plants, which can be constructed and equipped almost anywhere at short notice. But whatever the precise situation in practice, if the company has now a clear picture of what it requires it can then determine the location of its new plant.

A FACTORY LOCATION

Apart from the random influence of individual situations, such as a site at a bargain price or the preference of a com-pany chairman to have his new factory in a congenial area, near his private home – disregarding such cases – it is possible to discern three major determinants in factory location.

a Industrial geography.
b Government influence.
c Existing company plants.

a Industrial geography

A number of factors may be considered here, and to some extent they are likely to conflict with each other. The importance of a particular factor to a company depends on the industry within which it operates and on the technology of its production processes. It may be able to disregard

factors which in other industries could be of prime importance, and vice versa. There are instances where one factor
is of such importance that the others scarcely figure in the
decision-making process. In other cases the competing factors may be so well balanced that the choice of location is
based on marginal arguments.

i   Raw material supplies

Where raw materials are required in bulk and, at the
point of supply, they are available at a comparatively low
cost, then there is a strong case for locating a plant close to
their source. For instance, the beet sugar factories of the
British Sugar Corporation are located in East Anglia within the farming districts, where the beet is an important cash
crop. Another illustration is the location of the new Wiggins
Teape pulp mill near Fort William, Scotland, which ack-
nowledges the growing importance of reafforestation in that
part of the country.

ii   Availability of power

Where there is no exceptional power requirement for
production processes, the need to be located near a prime
source of power is no longer serious. There are, however,
cases, such as with aluminium smelting, where the economics of bulk electric power use require close proximity to,
and preferably control of, a cheap source of energy.

iii   Availability of suitable labour

The geographic disposition of labour skills is an important aspect, particularly where production has a high and
skilled labour content. Suitable skilled labour may be
largely concentrated in one or two towns or areas, such as
shoemaking in the Northampton/Leicester area or, as already mentioned, hatmaking in Luton. Of course, this need
not prevent a company setting up anywhere else and, if
necessary, importing suitable key personnel. Such a proposition needs, however, to be studied explicitly so that the
company knows the implications of setting up outside the
established sources of labour. Indeed, from a labour relations point of view it might be better at times to start somewhere removed from entrenched attitudes. On the other

hand, where there is a strong trade union influence on admission to crafts or apprenticeships, the required numbers of craft workers may just not exist in a new area.

iv Transport facilities

The availability of suitable transport facilities can be assessed both in broad geographic and in detailed local terms. For example, if the bulk of the raw material comes from abroad, as is the case with crude oil, then there is a strong argument for locating the oil refinery at the water's edge – as near as possible to the main tanker routes. This is not only important for incoming transport but also for subsequent distribution of the refined products by coastal tankers. For instance, the erection of oil refineries at Milford Haven, Pembrokeshire, has been largely due to deep-water anchoring facilities for oil tankers above 80,000 tons. The recent development of such tankers and the associated building of these refineries reflect the changes in oil transport economics which now favour the larger vessels. Another interesting example is the location of many of the East London furniture factories, which has often been governed by local lighterage traffic bringing imported timbers from the Port of London.

Where transport costs are substantial, either on the input or the output side of the production unit, it is important to make a careful study of all the feasible transport facilities and their respective costs before commitment to a definite location.

v Proximity of markets

The nature, concentration, and size of a market is a strong factor in the location of a new plant. In some cases, such as with the petrochemical and tonnage oxygen industries, the customer is at times literally just over the fence, and all that is needed is a short pipeline to deliver the plant output – with an agreed metering instrument of course! Such special situations are usually based on, and are the result of, long-term forward contracts. Proximity here may also have strong technological advantages. Apart from such instances, the more general argument is based on the reduction of delivery costs and times and on being near to a large number of customers. Where the fashion element is strong and a close knowledge of market moves and moods is important, then proximity has special advantages.

vi Related industries

In some cases the choice of factory location may be influenced by the distribution of related industries, which could be customers, suppliers, or subcontractors. For instance, in the Lancashire and Yorkshire textile industries, where production processes for cloth manufacture are still to some extent divided by ownership along traditional lines, this factor has retained some force. Similarly, the emphasis in the Birmingham/Coventry area on the motor industry, with attendant component manufacturers, light general engineering, and toolmaking, offers in some cases an attractive background which is also reflected in labour composition and availability, training facilities, and institutional support.

b **Government influence**

So far we have presumed that in our choice of location for a new production unit we could set up anywhere in the United Kingdom, as suggested by economic advantage. Such a free choice has become unrealistic, and government influence must be accepted as a fact of life. Government in this context includes both central and local government, and influence could be either in terms of support or restraint.

i Industrial development control

One form of restraint which affects the location of industry is the control of industrial building developments. The Board of Trade has the statutory authority to grant or to refuse industrial development certificates. These certificates are required to support planning applications for the erection, re-erection, extension, or alteration of an industrial building, or to turn a non-industrial building into an industrial one, if the proposed development, either by itself or together with any related development, is in excess of the prescribed exemption limits (in 1968 – 3,000 sq ft in the London, South-Eastern, and Midland regions; and 5,000 sq ft in the remainder of the country). This means that all developments, except the very minor schemes, are under statutory geographical control. In considering applications for industrial development certificates, the Board of Trade is required to have regard to the need for providing employment in the Development Areas. In practice, this means that a certificate is unlikely to be issued unless it can be shown that the proposed development cannot reasonably be undertaken there.

The preparation of the case for a particular factory location, to the satisfaction of the Board of Trade, has thus become an essential part of the initial staff work.

ii   Development areas

These areas are scheduled districts under the Local Employment Act 1960, where there is a special need to provide more employment. They include, typically, North-West Scotland, Clydeside, North-East England, Merseyside, part of North and South Wales, areas of Devon and Cornwall, as well as Northern Ireland. Government influence is here in the form of encouragement to counteract the economic and social decline of these areas because of structural industrial changes. Assistance under the 1960 and 1963 Local Employment Acts comes in a number of different ways. There is, of course, the growing differentiation between the development areas and the rest of the country in general economic planning and financial legislation, as may be noted, typically, from the 1968 Finance Act. The nature and scale of the incentives tend to vary with time, but the following is broadly the spring 1968 position.

Investment grants.   These amount to 45 per cent of the cost of new plant and machinery, as compared to 25 per cent for the rest of the country. (40 per cent and 20 per cent respectively after January 1st, 1969.)

Free depreciation.   Facilities exist under the 1963 Finance Act to write off capital expenditure on qualifying plant and machinery at whatever rate chosen.

New Board of Trade factories.   For rent or purchase at moderate cost.

Building grants. Up to 25 per cent of the cost of erecting or extending buildings.

Machinery grants. Up to 10 per cent of the cost of acquiring and installing plant and machinery.

Loans and grants for general expenditure.

Regional Employment Premium. A subvention of 30*s* per man per week.

Selective Employment Premium. This provides for a premium of 7*s* 6*d* per man per week within the framework of the Selective Employment Tax system.

Additional training grants. Up to £10 per week may be claimed in respect of each worker under training.

One might have expected, with all this wealth of assistance, that industry would have flocked into the development areas. Without doubt, there has been a considerable growth of new industries there, and this trend may continue. On the other hand, those responsible for the siting of the new production unit must consider the possible disadvantages of such a location. With some areas, extra transport or transhipment charges and remoteness from major markets are significant factors; also regional industrial attitudes are important, and these may impinge on production costs. A particular development, in this context, is with the larger industrial groups with factories in several parts of the country. There is the tendency – other things equal – for more of their expansion schemes to be located in those factories which a company already operates in development areas.

c **Existing company plants**

With the continuous process of amalgamation and company takeover, the approach to a new factory location, as part of a group strategy, is becoming increasingly important. The new plant location could be considerably affected by the disposition of other existing factories. It is important also to consider the nature and problems of management control, the disposition of staff resources, group transport problems, and the division of work between the various production plants. Are the plants entirely self-contained in their production, or should they be integrated with each other? Special marketing or distribution/transport problems may also be important, such as with can-making or bottle manufacture, where output is bulky in relation to value and the markets are widespread.

There is no difference here, in principle, between a large group and a one-factory type of business; but the complexity of the situation is increased and the interaction effects between the various production plants must be taken into account.

B FACTORY SITE ANALYSIS

When the decision as to general location has been taken the company will proceed to investigate promising sites for its prospective production units. It may, of course, have already made some initial inquiries. The acquisition of a site is in many respects similar to the purchase of a private house. The site may be free- or leasehold; it may have all sorts of restrictive covenants and encumbrances. Its proposition will have to be related to the company's specification, which, in turn, will reflect a transcription of immediate and possibly longer-term production plans.

a The 'rent, buy, or build' decision

In its quest for a suitable production unit the company may have to decide between the purchase or the tenancy of existing premises or the construction of its own factory. Where the production processes are specialized and services requirements are exceptional, the company may have to build its own factory to get the appropriate layout and building fabric. Where its needs are less exacting, existing premises may be suitable or adapted at moderate costs. New factory premises may be provided by the Board of Trade, local councils, new town corporations, industrial estates, or private developers. Apart from the possible immediate occupation, the advantage with this type of proposition is that with such premises goes the usual planning consent for industrial use, which cannot otherwise necessarily be taken for granted. For the rest, the attractiveness of such an arrangement is a function of price and commercial terms.

b Planning permission

Where a company intends to construct its own factory on a new site or wishes to expand on an existing one, it will require planning permission from the appropriate local authorities under the Town and Country Planning Act 1962. If planning consent is withheld and the appeal rejected the company may be forced to look for another site. Even if granted, the consent may be with a number of stipulations which could affect the arrangement and layout of the factory buildings. In addition, the company will have to conform to byelaws, building and fire regulations, etc, which may also affect the construction and concept of the new plant.

c Site analysis

Quite apart from the commercial and planning aspects, the evaluation of a particular site will require an analysis of the following aspects:

i   *Adequacy of site area.*   While this may be obvious for immediate needs, the longer-term aspects in respect of future expansion may also be relevant. Adequacy is not only a matter of acreage but also of shape and contours.

ii *Soil characteristics.*   The slopes and levels are significant, particularly with river or tidal frontages. The load-bearing characteristics of the soil will also have to be ascertained where machine and building loads are heavy. If these characteristics are poor the building costs may be substantially increased because of piling and extra foundation work. Such additional investment, unfortunately, shows little visible return, but may be required just the same.

iii *Site services.*   Site services comprise gas, water, and electricity supplies, as well as effluent and drainage facilities. The physical presence or nearness of such utilities at the required amount, voltage, pressure, etc, is the first object of analysis. Where these services are not readily available at the required specification, then it will be necessary to estimate the anticipated capital costs of bringing them to the site, including such contributions asked for by the supplying authorities to make the desired services available. Where the cooling-water load is substantial, permission may be required from local river or canal authorities to extract water, and even this may be sufficient only to make up the losses of a recycling cooling-water system. The company could be involved in protracted negotiations and be required to install costly effluent treatment units before it may be permitted to discharge its effluents into the local drainage or river system.

iv *Immediate location.* The precise location of the plot in relation to local transport facilities will be important. Main-road access, railway spurs, a canal or river frontage simplify the handling of incoming and outgoing goods traffic, particularly if it is bulky. Again, if the site is inaccessible it will be correspondingly less attractive to work there.

There are a number of other points to consider, such as the type and suitability of existing buildings, if any, but this will be developed further in Chapter Six. The main argument put forward here is to stress the need for careful analysis, both of location and site, when planning production on an overall basis, if this involves the building of a new factory.

3 DETAIL OPERATION PLANNING

Once the factory is established and equipped and the plant is a going concern, the day-to-day planning work will be of a more routine nature. Within the overall production planning framework already outlined it will be the task of the planning engineer to resolve the detailed aspects of every individual operation. He will not normally carry out all the work involved – for instance, he may use much of the data provided by the work study engineer – but he is regarded as responsible for the effectiveness of the planning task. This primarily hinges around the production order or work sheet. When an instruction is released from the works office to the production departments for the manufacture, say, of a batch of components or the assembly of a product, then the production order will serve as the technical master document. It will give the precise data or instructions for the completion of the work in hand, so that any responsible supervisor or operator knows what requires to be done. In this form, the production order can be conveniently expanded into a scheduling and production control document by leaving convenient space for authorizations, quantities, target or schedule dates, inspection and reject entries, etc.

The development of a production order sheet is part of the systems design for a production unit, and the form of the order should reflect the needs of a given work situation. The following details are typical of a production order used in the engineering and allied industries, primarily on small or large volume batch production:

PART OR ASSEMBLY NAME;

PART OR ASSEMBLY DRAWING REFERENCE;

PART OR ASSEMBLY NUMBER;

ASSEMBLY OR COMPONENT LIST REFERENCE;

MATERIAL DESCRIPTION AND CODE REFERENCE;

MATERIAL USAGE PER STANDARD QUANTITY
    OF PRODUCTION;

PRODUCT GROUP OR MODEL REFERENCE;

EFFECTIVE DATE OF INTRODUCTION;

RESPONSIBILITY FOR DOCUMENT;

AUTHORIZATION OF DOCUMENT ISSUE;

REFERENCE TO PREVIOUS OR SUPERSEDED
    DOCUMENTS;

MINIMUM ECONOMIC BATCH QUANTITIES;

OPERATION NUMBERS (given in production sequence);

OPERATION DESCRIPTION (similarly sequenced);

MACHINE NAME;

MACHINE NUMBER;

TOOL AND GAUGE DESCRIPTION;

TOOL AND GAUGE NUMBERS;

TOOL AND GAUGE LOCATION (where necessary);

OPERATION SETTING TIMES (stated, as appropriate,
    for each operation);

OPERATING SPEEDS AND FEEDS (stated, as appropriate, for each operation);

LABOUR GRADE (against each operation, where necessary);

RECTIFICATION AND SCRAP;

DOCUMENT DISTRIBUTION.

With such a document, the sequencing of the respective operations, with all the appropriate information specified at each stage, will give the physical routing of the work covered by the production order.

The detailed preparation of the technical master documents could overemphasize the clerical component of the work involved. Such documents are, however, only a summation of the planning activities and the decisions reached. Consider a typical example where the machining operations for a metal component are under investigation. Firstly, the planning engineer would appraise the physical characteristics of the part, ie, its dimensions, shape, and weight. He could then visualize the size of machine required for the various operations to be performed. The size of machines here is not in terms of physical dimensions, but relates to work-holding capacity. Secondly, he would evaluate the material in terms of its cutting or forming properties because this will govern the rate at which the operations may physically proceed and, by implication, determine the rate of output. It will also affect the choice of his tool materials, the design of the tools themselves, and the wear to be expected in operation. In turn, this will have repercussions on tool maintenance costs and possible production stoppages if tools have to be reconditioned frequently. Thirdly, he may use the intermediate component shape for holding or securing the part under operation. Fourthly, he will look at the condition in which the raw material or rough components are received. For instance, there could be a need for preparatory or cleaning operations. Perhaps more often, the planning engineer will determine the precise goods-inward specification, as part of the overall process planning. In the same manner he will also be concerned with the final

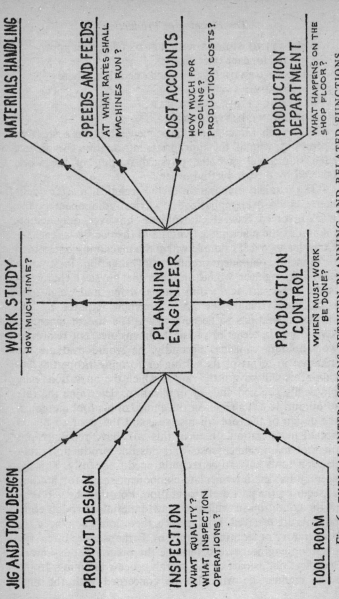

JIG AND TOOL DESIGN

PRODUCT DESIGN

INSPECTION
WHAT QUALITY?
WHAT INSPECTION
OPERATIONS?

TOOL ROOM

WORK STUDY
HOW MUCH TIME?

PLANNING ENGINEER

PRODUCTION CONTROL
WHEN MUST WORK BE DONE?

MATERIALS HANDLING

SPEEDS AND FEEDS
AT WHAT RATES SHALL MACHINES RUN?

COST ACCOUNTS
HOW MUCH FOR TOOLING? PRODUCTION COSTS?

PRODUCTION DEPARTMENT
WHAT HAPPENS ON THE SHOP FLOOR?

Fig. 6 TYPICAL INTERACTIONS BETWEEN PLANNING AND RELATED FUNCTIONS

tolerances specified on the component drawing, because these will determine the type of equipment to which the component will have to be routed. The sixth point will reflect his knowledge of machining operations; he will know or establish which sequence in practice is preferable on economic and technical grounds; which operations can be performed either simultaneously or in close succession on the same machine. He will also anticipate the effect such operations will have on the component material itself and whether any corrective treatment is called for. Lastly, the planning engineer will be interested in the quantities to be handled, for obviously this determines the degree of refinement and expenditure that can be accepted in the preparation of the component's manufacture.

Having thus gathered all the necessary facts, it will now be possible to look at existing machinery and to decide which shall be used. Similarly, the jig and tool drawing office can be told what to design and the various other related departments can be given their terms of reference. In this way the planning engineer will gather all specialist contributions and appropriately develop the production master data. Fig. 6 shows in a diagrammatic way the various relationships between the planning engineer and other departments which influence or contribute to his work.

FURTHER READING

S. Eilon: *Elements of Production Planning and Control*, Macmillan, 1962.

CHAPTER FOUR

The Nature of Production Processes

The variety of different production processes may be bewildering at first glance when, for instance, one compares an oil refinery with a car-assembly plant or a precision machine shop with a large clothing factory. This is to be expected because the diversity and range of technological attainment is the result of a division of labour and specialist developments. Nevertheless, in large-scale production particularly one can trace the continuing association of the main engineering disciplines – especially mechanical, electrical, electronic and chemical engineering – with various branches of science, such as polymer chemistry, physics, metallurgy.

In a book which is primarily concerned with the organization and management of production no justice can be done to the many technical aspects of even a single production process. It is presumed that a production manager has acquired the appropriate technical background by formal training and/or by suitable experience. To labour the obvious, he knows or should know what his plant looks like and how it works. But in many industries the same remark could equally apply to any competent maintenance fitter. In fact, the maintenance man's knowledge of the various plant details may be, and should be, superior to the production manager's. This is appropriate, because otherwise it could be argued that the production manager is not concentrating on his own responsibilities, which are in a wider context. Yet at the same time we note that the scope, cost, and complexity of production plant for the economic effectiveness of which the production manager is responsible is continuously increasing.

So what is then required from the production manager? He must have technical judgement, and this is based on broad background. He must appreciate the implications of technical development in terms of organization, human relations, and economics. He must have an overall view which covers the evolution of the plant with which he is concerned and which enables him to understand the trends that could affect its future. He must see the links, the common principles, and the projections of today's situation in respect of his production processes. His must be the integrated technical view.

1 THE EVOLUTION OF THE MACHINE

If we regard a machine as an apparatus for applying mechanical power, having several parts, each with its own definite function, we can then visualize a broad range of production equipment that could fall into such a category. Developing such an approach, we can also regard a chemical or pharmaceutical plant, for instance, as an overall machine, for power is normally required to pump or to convey a product stream, even if only to move it to a reaction vessel, where the production process then becomes a function of the chemical properties of the materials involved. Although machines have been used by mankind now for several thousand years, it is only the changes of the last 180 years or so that are of interest; when the availability of regular power, other than that of the animal or human kind, transformed the scale and manner of production.

A MACHINE CHARACTERISTICS

Irrespective of whether we deal with a simple electric sewing-machine or a mammoth size paper-making unit, we can discern certain common characteristics in all production plant and, furthermore, we can classify such plant in terms of these characteristics. In this manner, comparison is possible and the effects of technical change can be visualized.

a Machine structure

This is the main machine framework which gives a particular unit its specific appearance and basic dimensions. It may be constructed in a number of ways, either cast, fabricated, or bolted. There is, however, the growing tendency to use standard 'building block' machine parts for the development of a range or group of machines. The design is governed by the forces to be transmitted, the rate of work required, and the accuracy of the work demanded. As a structure, it therefore requires the necessary strength, rigidity, and overall stability for the processes to be performed without hampering the combination of movements required in operation. Particularly important, with machines operating at any speed, is the avoidance of vibrations which could affect the accuracy and finish of the work handled.

b Power – source and transmission

In most cases, the power supplied to production equipment is electric, although steam turbines or diesel engines may be appropriate in some special situations. Although there are still a number of old factories with extensive overhead (or under bench) shafting, the normal practice is to supply power to each individual machine, either down from the ceiling or up from cable ducts, cast or cut in the floor. The power comes to the machine via a central switch or connecting box from which the machine supplier has already connected to the main drives and other ancillary electrical equipment on the machine. A feature of modern production plant is the ever-growing number of small drives, either actuating accessories, control systems, or service feeds, such as oil or coolants, which are necessary for effective machine operation.

The power itself is transmitted, either directly or through gearboxes, to the operative part of the machine, with a clutch mechanism so arranged that the unit can be taken smoothly in and out of operation. The range of speeds and feeds that can be provided through a gearbox can either be composed of discrete steps, as with a car, or be infinitely variable. For standard production plant there may only be a need for three to four main speeds for the major drives.

c Work area

It is within this area that the actual production process takes place. The materials are transformed by tools; they are held in position by chucks, jigs, or clamps or, as in the case with plastic extrusion, they are moved by a screw through a die. Alternatively, material may be fed on to a component, such as with the winding of electric coils; or by deposition in a plating process. Operations may require linear motion in three planes or rotation around any of the three main coordinate axes. With some equipment, applied to the machining of heavy castings, the working area, encompassed by large traverse movements, may dwarf the operator. In other cases, such as with micro-electronic circuit manufacture, it may be properly visible only with a microscope. Again, some machines are designed for one operation only, with one work station. Others can perform a number of operations in quick succession with one work station, using tools actuated by a carefully controlled time cycle. Many special-purpose machines have a number of work stations, each performing a specified task and possibly incorporating within a given cycle holding operations allowing, say, for the cooling, heating, or drying of a work piece, if this is a necessary part of the process.

d Machine controls

There are many fields of production where the actual process has changed little, if at all, over a number of years. What has, however, changed appreciably may be the way in which such operations are actuated, controlled, and sequenced. Initially, it was the basic task of the operator to start, run, and stop his machine and to check, essentially by the application of his senses, that the machine performance was to his satisfaction. In highly repetitive work the extent of manual operation is diminishing; with increasing speeds, the manual component within a given work cycle tends to limit the rate of output, and repetitive movements are taken over by high-speed mechanisms. The discretionary element

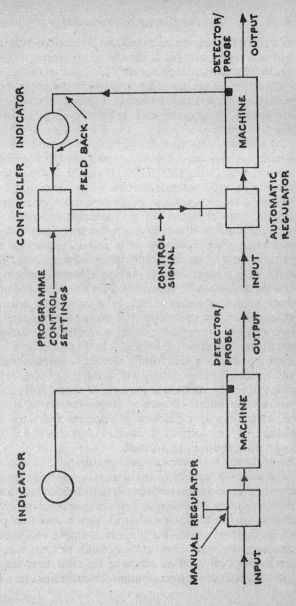

OPEN LOOP—OPERATOR CONTROL   CLOSED LOOP—AUTOMATIC CONTROL

Fig. 7 OPEN- AND CLOSED-LOOP CONTROL SYSTEMS

in a work task can be classified and transcribed into a control system. An over- or under-size component can be automatically ejected, no component at all can stop the machine; visible and, to the human eye, invisible defects can trip a deflecting or separating device. Indeed, a whole defect eventuality programme can be written into a machine control system.

In design, this is reflected by electric and electronic circuits, relays, cut-out switches, and sensing devices. The electric controls in turn may actuate (or be actuated by) pneumatic and hydraulic circuits, which, in turn, give rise to mechanical movement to position tools, open or shut clamps, transfer materials, etc. The extent and sequence of such movements is usually controlled by probes and interlock circuits which can be set to suit a specific task or be programmed to suit a variable range of such tasks. Physically, such controls may be housed separately in a control box or desk console, separated from the plant it controls. Such control systems reflect, in a cybernetic sense, the change from an open-loop to a closed-loop control. The operator, as a regulating unit, is replaced by automatic regulators, as shown graphically in Fig. 7. The machine itself monitors the data from a number of specified sources, and as long as such data is within the permissible range it takes no action. As soon as the data, however, drifts towards one of the limits of such a range, corrective action is initiated, such as the closing or opening of a valve or the change of an electrical resistance until the signal moves away from the limit in question.

e   Materials feed, storage, and removal

Where the feeding of material is a repetitive task and the scale of operation justifies the initial outlay, the loading process is often mechanized. In some cases, such as with the feeding of continuous metal strip from a coil to a power press, the feed device may be quite simple and cheap to construct. In other cases, gravity chutes or unit-dispensing mechanisms can feed an article at the right time sequence and offer it in the correct position. Transfer links can divert such articles as bottles or cans from conveyors to filling stations at the precise intervals and distances for high-speed filling. The careful registration and position control of each individual article is, of course, essential for high-speed work.

The storage of ancillary materials for the purpose of processing, such as inks, adhesives, solvents, plastic pellets, etc, may also be significant, as it could affect machine labour attendance and consistency of performance. The storage of such materials may, in turn, be linked with a general factory supply system which pipes or conveys automatically make-up quantities to a machine, in response to a low-level signal.

In principle, product removal is similar to materials feed, and in practice it is often simpler. The take off, whether by mechanical means or air ejection, is coordinated with the main machine process cycle, so as to avoid jamming and materials build-up. Frequently, the take off from one machine is linked with the feed to the next unit, and in this manner a transfer or automatic line, joining several machines, can be developed.

B MACHINE PERFORMANCE

In the same way as it is possible to analyse the physical concept of a machine, so it will be possible to dissect its performance. This, in turn, may hinge around two or three key aspects which justify the selection of a particular unit in the first place, or point to the subsequent development of further plant models.

a *Output rate*

The rate of production is understandably of prime interest, even if the machine is automatic and requires no operator attendance. While speeding up may be feasible by changing to a faster motor or modifying the transmission system, the limitations of mechanical design and/or the cost of such a conversion may make this unattractive. With an existing machine design and the previous application of work study, the scope for further improvement is limited. There may, however, in some cases be more scope with multi-unit production, where the machine structure permits a tool, for instance, to press out or to mould a number of units within the same work cycle.

b   Quality of work

The quality of work required, be it expressed in terms of dimensional accuracy, finish, or material specification, often determines plant selection, such as in metalworking, and it is possible here to overstate as well as to understate what is needed. A high-speed, high-quality machine may be the ideal, but its capital costs are then correspondingly heavy, even if a suitable machine of such a character exists. To be of economic worth, the quality of work must be maintained consistently over long periods, and although deterioration in performance may be expected over time and with extensive use, the plant performance specifications should be met, as long as the equipment has a book value, ie, until its notional working life has expired. The quality of work should also be achieved without an escalation of tooling costs and other preparatory expenses.

c   Labour attendance

The ideal plant is one that is switched on, either locally or remotely, and can then be forgotten about as far as its operation is concerned. While such plant exists, the majority of production equipment does require attendance of some sort. Attendance may be a one-man/one-machine relationship or a whole gang of labour serving one production unit. It also covers multi-machine operation, such as is typically found in the textile industries, where one girl may attend a battery of similar machines, and the near-automatic plant, where attendance becomes primarily a matter of dial watching and logbook entries. Attendance in the latter case is more on the fire brigade principle – to be immediately available when an alarm or emergency signal is given. Labour costs in such cases are more like a form of insurance premium. Of course, labour attendance is more than just a matter of numbers. The grade of labour and supervision required is also relevant. For instance, in the process industries members of the line management of production are much more closely involved with plant operation than they would be, say, in the engineering industries.

It is, of course, appreciated that in a situation of complex labour relations the manning of any plant is not solely governed by the technical machine requirements. In fact, a labour situation may be so overwhelming in a given context that technical requirements are all but ignored. The risk then is that plant manning becomes a function of bargaining and that operating labour economies are to some extent discounted.

An interesting development is the machine which operates in toxic, radioactive, or other hazardous areas, where no attendance is possible. This development is likely to become more significant in the future.

d Maintenance requirements

It is common experience that the maintenance requirements for a production plant can vary a good deal. The costs of maintenance can be evaluated in terms of maintenance time spent or spare parts inventories and standby plant, that has to be carried. The bigger the plant, the more costly becomes downtime, especially where the shutting-down and starting-up procedure results in further process losses. While increasing sophistication can bring its own technical risks, the relatively commonplace is by no means immune from failure in normal operation. One may also distinguish here between relatively routine maintenance requirements which can be handled by the user's maintenance section and those special cases which require a supplier's engineer in a great hurry at short notice. The experienced production manager respects proven plant!

e Services consumption

While this may not be quite so critical a factor in some of the metal-using fields, the process industries (chemicals, petrochemicals, pharmaceuticals) are more concerned with the services required by their various production units. The chief requirements are normally electric power, steam (at various pressures and temperatures), fuel gas, compressed air or inert gases, such as nitrogen, refrigerants, cooling water, etc. The consumption of such services is not only a matter of operating costs but may also involve substantial expenditures on ancillary capital equipment. Over the years, research and development has reduced the services consumption per given unit of output for many processes, but as the scale of manufacture has often increased more rapidly, the actual quantities involved have risen. Economy of services consumption is therefore a matter of close interest, particularly in those process fields where expenditure on such utilities could be a much heavier operating expense than direct labour costs.

2 THE NATURE OF AUTOMATION

Automation, as a subject, is widely referred to in general discussion, but its meaning in the context of production is not always clear. A review of the subject of automation, published in 1957 by the then Department of Scientific and Industrial Research (HMSO Publication), gives perhaps the most useful interpretation. Automation is regarded essentially as a confluence of the following:

a Transfer devices, which link individual machines into automatic production lines. These devices are associated with advanced techniques of materials handling and assembly.
b Automatic control over production processes.
c Automatic information processing and instruction giving by electronic computers.

Developing such a concept to its ultimate, an automatic factory will involve the automatic operation of the following:

a All essential working operations.
b Inspection and quality control systems.
c Product handling and warehousing.
d Product assembly.
e Central plant control.

Using such an interpretation, some of the earlier remarks in this chapter also refer to automated plant and, in practice, it may be difficult to decide when a machine or production unit is automated or not. A useful distinction can, however, be drawn between a basically conventional plant unit which has been automated and comparative equipment where automation was integrated as one of the basic design objectives. A helpful approach is also given by D. Foster[1], who explicitly differentiates between automation and mechanization. In his view, however sophisticated or integrated a plant may be, it is 'blind' if it can carry out only the mechanical tasks assigned to it. If, for instance, one of the parameters of a process, such as temperature or work quality, were to deteriorate it could not take note of it and make corresponding adjustments. A truly automated plant has a 'mind' which could evaluate the messages transmitted from its sensory devices, and take action accordingly.

A PROCESS CONTROL

Automatic process control can be applied to continuous and to batch, ie, discrete, processes. For instance, the nature of many of the chemical processes has facilitated automation, and the chemical industry has been accustomed to automatic control for many years. The manner of automation itself has continued to evolve and has become ever more sophisticated and comprehensive. A scheme of automation for a large chemical plant may now cost up to £500,000, and this outlay is considered worthwhile because it gives greater flexibility and better plant control, which in turn can be transcribed into quantified benefits, such as higher process yields, lower material and utilities costs.

Nature of control

1 *Local controllers*. This is the simplest form of automation. Every condition which requires control on the various parts of the process plant has local control units which sense the local conditions, and in response to predetermined signals or settings open and close valves or circuits to maintain a given set of process conditions. Where the plant is sizeable there may be problems of achieving an overall process balance because the control operations of one unit can unsettle the operation of other parts. Experienced and careful plant supervision is of importance here.

2 *Control rooms.* A large process plant is usually in the open, it occupies a substantial area, and many of the reaction vessels or columns may be over 100 ft high. Unless such a plant is swamped with operators, there is a need for a central control area, where the required process information is gathered, indicated, and recorded, and where emergency signals and alarms denote the failure of a particular control function. Production programmes are initiated by the remote setting of the local control units, with manual overrides where special adjustments are required with a programme change.

3 *Multi-point scanning and data handling systems.* Anyone who has been to the control room of a large modern chemical plant or power station will be impressed by the great number of instrument dials and recorders which tell the control supervisor what is happening to his plant at any given moment. To transmit such a great variety of data from a process area, economically and accurately, it is possible to use a single transmission system with input and output scanners, in the process and control-room areas respectively, which match a message emanating from a particular sensing point with its corresponding control-room instrument. For the purpose of transmission, the sensing-point message which will be in the form of an amplitude (analogue) signal will be transcribed into a digital (pulse) code.

The visually indicated data can be simultaneously recorded on charts which show in graphical form either a particular reading or a group of observations, taken to a preset time cycle from a number of different points. Alternatively, all the various data can be fed into a data-logging unit which collates all the messages received and prints them out simultaneously on standard plant log sheets. With a large process unit the data thus made available can be somewhat overwhelming, and the print-out may be confined only to those measurements which deviate by more than a set amount from the target or control data.

4 *Computer-controlled process plants.* There are various

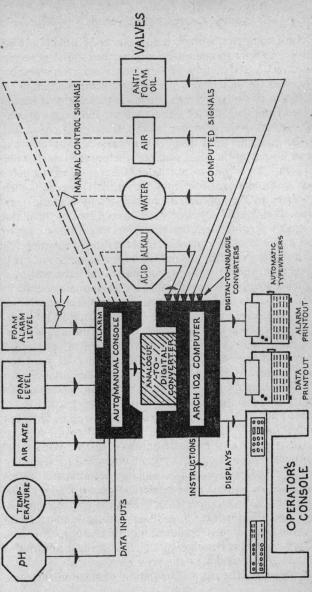

Fig. 8 SIMPLIFIED DIRECT DIGITAL CONTROL SYSTEM FOR A BATCH FERMENTATION PROCESS
By courtesy of Elliott-Automation Ltd

levels of computer control, but in this book it will only be possible to refer to one of the simpler forms. The principle of a direct digital control structure for a batch fermentation process as shown in Fig. 8 gives a convenient illustration.

It will be noted from the diagram that the data inputs are fed from the detector into an auto-manual control console located in the computer room. The signals are routed to the computer and also to instruments, thus giving a visual display of the plant situation. Before the signals enter the computer they are converted into a corresponding pulse code by an analogue-to-digital converter. This code is then processed by the appropriate control equation in the computer. This control equation is, of course, part of the initial computer programme, when it receives its instructions as to how it should run the plant. The answer to the equation is a control signal for the associated valve on the plant. This signal from the control equation has to be translated by a digital-to-analogue converter into a corresponding electrical level, which in turn generates the pneumatic signal that moves the valve to its desired position. An automatic type-writer takes computer instructions for the continuous print-out of control data, while a separate 'alarm' typewriter concentrates on data which is detected outside predetermined limits. A separate console enables the duty operator to make simple programme changes, such as altering set points or alarm limits. The computer in this particular example handles altogether 50 fermentation vessels with 114 control loops.

B NUMERICALLY CONTROLLED MACHINE TOOLS

While a process plant is basically designed for a specific group of process operations, which in technological terms may be quite restricted, the numerically controlled machine tools, now coming into greater use in the engineering, aircraft, and allied industries, combine automatic control with operational flexibility. To use a tailoring analogy, automatic process control is bespoke, numerically controlled machine tools are for immediate use.

In essence, the manual operation of standard machine

tools, such as milling machines, jig borers, drills, lathes, etc, is taken over by automatic control. The machine tool has a control and actuating unit which works to the instructions of a prepared programme. The programme may be fed to the control console by punched cards, paper or magnetic tape, or plug boards, depending on the control system in use. The nature of the numerically controlled operation itself falls into two major subdivisions:

1 Continuous path control or 'contouring', where the position and speed of the work tool is controlled for all motions within the work cycle.

2 'Point-to-Point' or positioning systems, where the control is discrete over specific operations, such as the drilling or tapping of holes. The programmed movement from one workpoint location to the next is at a predetermined machine speed, which is not normally under control instructions.

The more versatile machine tools provide positional control in terms of the three coordinate axes. This is linear motion, which can be compounded for the machining of complex shapes. For specific applications it is also possible to have numerical control in terms of rotational movement about given axes.

A feature with some of the more complex machine tools is the large number of different tools, such as drill, reamers, cutters, etc, that can be housed in the machine turrets or magazines and which can be moved to the operating positions, as required by the programmed instructions. It is possible to have fifty or more different tools available on some of the latest machines, and these are normally 'preset' on separate fixtures to reduce the changeover time on the equipment. The actual machining operations are related to datum lines on the workpiece, and the positioning accuracy of numerically controlled machines corresponds to equivalent conventional machines on production work. Compensation for tool wear and automatic shut down, should there be a 'drift' in excess of the permitted tolerances, reduce the risk of spoilt work.

The preparation of the required programmes is part of the production-planning function. Assuming that a given work task is suitable for numerically controlled machining – this may be a function of quantity – the sequence of operations is then determined. Such a sequence could be different from that specified for an equivalent conventional machine. The planning engineer fixes datum lines and loading points, specifies machining operations and tools, by suitable code numbers, and states the required coordinate positions and movements. These can then be transcribed, either by manual tape preparation or by the computer, into the actual machine instructions. The faster computer operation becomes more attractive as the complexity of the programme increases, as it can also carry out all the detail calculations and therefore substantially reduce the routine drawing-office work. Completed programmes, after use, are suitably filed, to be readily available when the required work is called for again at a later date.

C MACHINE CENTRES

A development which is just becoming significant is the integration of a number of numerically controlled machine tools in the form of a machine centre. Such a centre, when fully automated, is computer controlled. The computer controls the machining operations as well as the handling and transfer of workpieces to and from the machines. To simplify operations and to reduce capital costs, there is usually a division of labour among the machines; some are on milling work, others concentrate on drilling operations or on boring, etc. The workpieces to be machined are set up on precision pallets which then are transferred and posted via the computer-controlled conveyor to the chosen machines for the desired range of operations. Automatic inspection machines may also be incorporated for quality control.

A typical illustration of such a machine centre is given in Williamson's account of the 'Molins System 24'[2].

3 THE IMPLICATIONS OF AUTOMATION

While it may well be argued that in the United Kingdom there is an inadequate rate of technical change and that the application of automation to production processes is not fast enough, there is nevertheless an underlying secular trend in this direction. It is strong in the newer industries which themselves are the product of technical innovation and it is commonplace in some of the process industries. The changes in the future are likely to be in the more labour-intensive industries, such as light engineering, motor vehicles, shipbuilding, etc. Because of the larger labour forces that will be affected, labour relations and social changes will be correspondingly more critical.

The development of automation in production processes is, of course, complemented by the automation of clerical procedures, information systems, and the general use of the computer as a tool of organization and management control. The changes are on several fronts; they affect the office, the warehouse, and the shop floor. Furthermore, such changes are not necessarily received with great enthusiasm by those immediately affected and, in order to minimize the consequent stresses that may be set up within a manufacturing organization, there will be a great need for intelligent anticipation, careful planning, and managerial skill. Complex and expensive tools, if they are going to be of any financial benefit to a company, will require a thorough and scientific approach, be it a feasibility study, systems analysis, or operational control. Scientific method, mathematical techniques, thoroughness of preparation, and careful planning will have an increasing emphasis, and this will gradually change the 'flavour' of production management in the years to come. The success in economic and social terms of such changes in methods and tone will also depend on the attitude of those affected. The fear that 'the computer will displace us' is of the same kind as that which prompted the Luddites to destroy machinery in the early nineteenth century. A new social and industrial philosophy needs to be evolved – one which is acceptable not just to the computer expert and his management but also to the man on the shop floor and his union.

Apart from such overall implications, there are a number of specific aspects that deserve mention:

Growth of capital investments

The economist has long been familiar with the secular trend in industrial societies, for the capital component in production to grow more rapidly than the labour component. This largely reflects some of the technological developments, already referred to. From a company point of view, progress will mean continuous and substantial investment, and the financial resources required for this may militate against the small business, unless it is in a particularly favoured position. The firm will also require an organization, attuned to investment projects, with a number of people taken out of the day-to-day preoccupations. The assimilation process, as far as new plant and equipment is concerned, can in no way be taken for granted.

Systems and procedures

Much of the organizational dislocation and subsequent disenchantment with computers, numerically-controlled machine tools, and other automated equipment arises from insufficient environmental preparation. The scope, opportunities, and the desired role of automation must be clearly defined, whatever the particular situation. Where such preparatory work is undertaken methodically, it is likely to question the form of the existing organization, its procedures and information flow, the disposition of responsibilities, etc. In many instances the existing organizational framework developed on an *ad hoc* basis. Even where deeper analysis contributed to the development of the existing systems, the presumptions on which these were based are likely to be affected by the character of Electronic Data Processing (EDP).

Successful automation is based on systems analysis and design. The whole situation and the basic objectives must be assessed and if necessary be restated. Arising from such a total view which now embraces automation, new systems can then be evolved which integrate the contributions and structures of the various components required for their operation. In essence, manufacturing organization will have to change for the effective utilization of automation.

Changes in employee patterns

The move towards automation will bring with it a range of new skills and staff. There is a call for the systems engineer and analyst, the computer programmer and the production engineer, capable of design and planning for automated processes. High-quality specialists in these fast-developing areas are scarce; the supply and demand situation not only makes them expensive but also has side effects on the company's general salary structure. Similarly, on the plant side, the new maintenance commitments require a different level of attendance. The well-tried combination of craft skill and practical commonsense which has for so long characterized the resourceful approach of the maintenance gang is no longer adequate. Broadly trained professional engineering resources and technicians' skills will have to support and strengthen the maintenance function.

On the operating side there will be more displacement of production labour. As automatic plant will need less routine supervision, multi-machine or plant attendance will become more widespread. The manual work content, the physical tasks, will diminish, and this will also reduce the manual skills required in routine operation. The operator will become more of a dial watcher and standby man. Such changes in work patterns, and the ensuing redundancies, will stress the need for the retraining and rehabilitation of larger groups of workers. Similar trends may also be noted in respect of clerical labour, but as there has been a long-term growth in indirect 'white collar' employment, automation is not likely to make as drastic an impact here as on the shop floor. In fact, some of the financial disappointments with certain computer installations, that promised an overall reduction in clerical labour costs, are due to the redeployment of ostensibly redundant clerical labour on other work, which now somehow needed to be done.

On the whole, therefore, the number of indirect workers will increase and those directly working on production will further diminish. In some of the process industries the direct production workers are already in a minority. The 'white collar' staff man will grow in proportion, and the distinction between the staff man and the manual, hourly paid, employee may become less clear cut. This may well prompt a revision in industrial work-status classifications. Managers will control larger plants, but fewer people, and this will affect the whole structure of organization. The work rate will be governed by the plant-operating characteristics, and as it will depend less on the physical effort of the worker, this will have repercussions on incentive bonus and payments systems. Work study and measurement will be concerned more and more with indirect labour, which will form the greater part of the company's payroll.

Economic influences

The investments that will be required to achieve production automation will bring with them heavier depreciation charges, which in turn affect trading results. There will be a greater urge to ensure the full utilization of automatic plant. This phenomenon has already been noted in the increase of shift work, undertaken in industries where hitherto there was only limited economic pressure for such a development. To some extent this trend has been masked because of the lower labour requirements for automated plant, ie, the amount of plant on shift work has increased at a faster rate than the required personnel.

In many instances the hourly rate of production has increased, even if the precise process or work cycle has remained unaltered. Where the opportunity for general plant redesign has been taken, the improvement is often correspondingly greater. The most frequent improvements here are the elimination of operator delays, particularly with loading and unloading, preset tooling which avoids much of the idle machine time when setting up, automatic sensing devices, and high accuracy work repeatability, which have cut down scrap rates. The greater rate of output makes larger batch sizes more attractive and has increased the pressure for standardization, simplification, and work-group classification, better known as group technology.

Where process automation has been successful in large-scale manufacture, it has achieved substantial reductions in operating costs because of a larger output coupled with reduced labour requirements and better materials control. In the engineering industries some spectacular achievements in productivity and cost reduction have also been recorded, but the variety of work tasks and the still relatively limited experience in organizing numerically controlled production have made the economic advantages of automation here not yet as telling as they have become in the process industries.

REFERENCES

1 D. Foster: *Modern Automation*, Pitman, 1963.
2 D. T. N. Williamson: *System 24 – A New Concept of Manufacture*. 8th International Machine Tool Design and Research Conference, 1967. Pergamon.

FURTHER READING

D.S.I.R. *Automation*, H.M. Stationery Office, 1957.
G. H. DeGroat: *Metalworking Automation*, McGraw Hill, 1962.
A. H. Simon: *The Shape of Automation*, Harper and Row, 1965.
D. E. Greene: *Production Technology*, Chapman and Hall, 1962.

CHAPTER FIVE

The Quality of Production

'Each solderless connexion – as many as 20,000 in the multi-axis control systems – is tested with automatic test equipment to ensure proper wiring and positive contact.'

'Operated from a punched tape, programmed from a wiring table, it scans thousands of terminal connexions, one by one for continuity and extra wires.'

'If the tester detects faulty wiring a projection type readout display provides the circuit point number, tape block number, and whether it is a missing or extra wire.'

These statements illustrate the claim of 'designed-in reliability' by a well-known manufacturer of numerical control equipment for machine-tool applications. The stress on reliability in the brochure which contained these statements reflects some quality control requirements and user attitudes. These may conveniently be transcribed into the following questions:

1 How well made is the equipment?
2 How reliable will it be in its functional purpose? What safeguards has the supplier taken to ensure this reliability?
3 What problems shall we have as users, to keep the equipment in the desired state?
4 How long will the equipment remain usable for our purpose?

To give a reasoned answer to such questions requires a full consideration of what the quality of a particular product should be, and once this has been determined, how this level of quality should be planned for in terms of method, equipment, and organization, and how it should be implemented and maintained in production. Quality, when viewed in such a context, becomes as basic a consideration as the scale or method of manufacture. Such a concept is reinforced by the scale and cost of quality control, as products and production methods become increasingly complex.

This emphasis on quality and reliability is not only a matter of company policy and planning but has also become of national interest, as shown by the 1967 'National Quality and Reliability Year'. Official support for this reflects the concern that British industry is not as competitive as it could be on these counts which, particularly with manufactured equipment, are of importance to potential customers abroad, and therefore have long-term implications on our international trading position.

Before assessing the relevance of quality to production management it will be desirable to define the main terms of discussion.

Quality itself can be regarded as a general degree of excellence of a given product. It concerns itself with the product's nature, characteristics, and features. If we represented quality on an 'excellence scale' high quality would be somewhere near the top and low quality correspondingly at the other end. Such a total concept of excellence can, in turn, be divided into a number of constituents, such as strength, work finish, design, etc, and similar excellence scales may be drawn up for these. In such a way we can analyse the quality of a given product; it may score well in some respects, and could be mediocre in other directions. A weighted summation of such constituent assessments can give us an indication of quality. It must be noted here that quality may be quantifiable in some respects, but subjective and incapable of measurement in others. There is also the interrelationship between the observer and the product, for when he sees some feature which in his mind suggests a substantial work content he may regard this – rightly or wrongly – as an indication of quality.

Reliability refers to the dependability of a device or a machine to carry out a specified task, and to repeat such tasks when activated. It is an indication of functional competence, and as such it can be measured in terms of use value by the duration of the acceptable performance.

Quality Control is responsible for the provision of the correct product quality to the customer, consistent with minimum resource use. This description includes the determination and specification of such quality standards, as well as their maintenance.

1 COMPANY QUALITY POLICIES

The reader will recall the various product policy aspects discussed in Chapter Two. Product quality is an important policy consideration, as it affects the company's markets and the way in which it makes its living. A company can aim at a high-quality, high-price but low-quantity market, or at a modest-quality, competitive-price, large-volume business. Endless variations between these concepts are possible, depending on the specific product or company policy. Naturally, the chosen product policy, reflecting the company's marketing strategy, will determine and provide the terms of reference for the required quality-control effort. There are also quite a number of cases where a company does not really have a choice as to quality in the conduct of its business. In the electronic, aircraft, or guided-missile business, for instance, the contract specifications on quality and performance are by their nature exacting and give little room for policy discretion.

When the company has resolved its approach to the market in terms of strategy, product specifications, and advertising it will then have to stand the challenge of competition. In a dynamic state policies, framed within the context of a particular business situation, may require periodic review and possibly revision. But in the intervening periods policy guidance on quality may encourage its continuous improvement without an increase in cost or price, or alternatively, furnish the same quality at a lower price to the consumer. Although resale price maintenance has had no encouragement from the Courts in recent years, there are still areas in which competition hinges not so much on price, as on service and product quality. Indeed, a good deal of the research and development expenditure incurred by some companies on already well-established products is essentially to improve or maintain their market standing, in terms of quality and reliability.

In practice, much of the raw material for the policy development is in the form of feedback information from suppliers and customers. This can come as field reports from the sales department, defect or rejection notes from purchasing or production, or from the occasional desperate letter to the managing director. In some industries, such as in packaging, the feedback is quite formalized; new lines are sample tested by the customer as a matter of routine for quality, and his laboratory reports give the supplier both comment and objective data. There is further scope for such closer association on quality between supplier and user. In the broader market setting the growth of consumer associations, with their widely publicized reports, has also become significant.

Also integral with the company's quality policies is its view on overall quality control. Where this is not specified by an outside body, and this is still the majority of cases, it has to decide the form and the extent of its quality-control system. It has the choice of what Davies and McCarthy[1] call the whole range of alternatives between cheap sloppiness and expensive overdiligence. How far shall we take our quality control? How much money, or where relevant, what proportion of our turnover shall we spend on it? These are difficult questions to answer not only because of the economic aspects but because they involve an appraisal of goodwill and customer relationships, both of which are intangible and variable. It might, for instance, be possible to spend £100 on free and ungrudging replacements, and this could save £1,000 in corresponding quality-control costs. Yet most companies would hesitate to secure such savings at the expense of goodwill. Where a business has paid little attention to quality control, it tends, sooner or later, to get into trouble with some of its more important customers and will pay for it in terms of reputation and turnover. Where it manages to retain the customers and extricate itself from a difficult situation, it tends for a while to over-inspect and control, which does not help its production costs. Such gyrations reflect lack of policy.

In essence, then, a concept of quality control requires economic decision-making. It is concerned with how much of the company's resources are to be used to achieve a certain standard of quality, how much risk may be taken, and the likely costs of a possible failure.

2 PLANNING FOR QUALITY CONTROL

Taking the company's quality policies as a basis, it will now be possible to plan a quality-control system. In this respect the development of quality control is similar to production planning, and just as quality-control policies have to be integrated with manufacturing policies, as part of the overall company view, so the quality-control system will also have to be integrated with the manufacturing system. It cannot be planned in isolation, and it is only for the convenience of analysis that it is segregated in description. Where the size of the business warrants it, a quality-control manager may be responsible for the development and integration of quality control within the company's operations. In smaller establishments quality control may be devised jointly by a production technologist and those responsible for routine inspection or control. The setting up of a quality-control system, within the company framework, can be represented diagrammatically, as shown in Fig. 9. It will not, however, always be possible to predict the precise control requirements for a new product, and much of the value of prototype

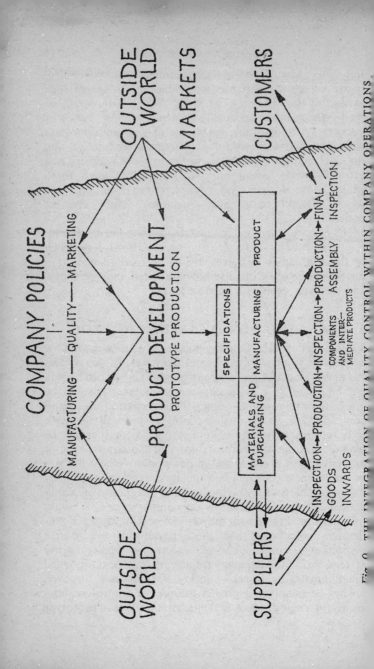

Fig. 9. THE INTEGRATION OF QUALITY CONTROL WITHIN COMPANY OPERATIONS

testing and pre-production evaluation lies in the guidance which such experience makes available for quality-control planning.

In the planning of the quality-control system for a given product or process an inspection operations process chart can be prepared similar in character to the operations process chart already described in Chapter Three. The product and its constituents can then be scrutinized for quality requirements. Some of these are functional, ie, they are part of the product specification and necessary for the proper use of the article by the customer. Others are essential for economy and effectiveness in production, such as precise component machining tolerances which make for subsequent ease of assembly. Such scrutiny of quality requirements also takes note of the characteristics of the existing production plant or any equipment that is likely to be installed. Where the accuracy achieved by a piece of production equipment is near the limit of acceptability, it may be advisable in some cases to give such a machine special inspection attention. It is not always a matter of replacing the machine or reconditioning it. A proper economic and quantified decision process assesses the cost of extra inspection, and if this is modest over the conceived time scale in relation to the alternatives available, then such extra inspection may be preferable.

An analysis of inspection requirements can usefully be based on the following questioning procedure, which reflects the well-known work-study approach:

a   Why inspect? There is no point spending time and money to look at or to measure something unless we get some useful information as a result; and information is useful only when it tells us what to do at the time of inspection, in terms of adjustment or correction.

b   When should we inspect? This is also linked with the question of how many inspection points there should be in the production process. Inspection work costs time and money, it lengthens the total production cycle, adds to administration and work in progress. Wish we could dispense with it! Yet, on the other hand, the further a production task proceeds, the more money is spent on it, the added value is the greater, and the losses are corresponding when the article has to be scrapped at a later stage. The nature of machining processes on large and expensive castings may make inspections imperative after every operation; in other cases it could be worth the risk to make checks only after a group of operations. Much depends here on the ease and costs of rectification. The precise determination as to when an inspection is required – whether, for example, it should be after operation No 3 or No 5 – depends on the nature of the individual operations and their relationships, the plant in question, and, where applicable, on the extent of self-regulation or automatic correction built into the equipment.

c How should the inspection be carried out? Once the need and sequence position of an inspection operation has been determined, the nature of the task itself can then be defined in terms of process requirements. Such requirements may be stated in linear terms, such as in dimensional tolerances, or terms of purity, oxygen content, melt index, material hardness. Once these process-inspection needs have been defined, then the manner in which the task may be carried out and what equipment is called for will in most cases also crystallize. On the other hand, with novel production processes there may be inspection or quality-assurance problems which are just as awkward to resolve as some production engineering or materials-handling difficulties. When the inspection routine has been defined, when jigs or tools have been designed and manufactured, when the appropriate test and ancillary equipment has been procured and proven for the purpose, then the inspection process is best put into writing, not only for the purpose of inspector training and continuity but also to assist with possible future investigations into production problems. There is much to be said for the introduction of standard inspection planning sheets which give the sequence of the inspection steps and define the equipment and specify which parts can be updated, when required.

d Who should carry out the inspection? One basic aspect touched by such a question is whether production workers or full-time inspectors should carry out the work. There are a number of wider management implications to this point which will be discussed separately. But apart from this, the nature and specification of the inspection task will provide a technical guide. There are a number of inspection grades, requiring different skills, experiences, and aptitudes, particularly in large engineering or motorcar factories, where hundreds of inspectors might be on the payroll. An inspection task can be assessed by job-evaluation techniques – like any production job – and an appropriate job grade can be fixed for it. Needless to say, some inspection tasks are routine, semi-manual, monotonous, and repetitive; others require the careful use of high-grade and expensive specialist equipment; and others again call for the application of statistical control techniques, which in turn demand analytical and intellectual effort.

e Where should the inspection work be carried out? There is a strong attraction to carry out all inspection and quality-control work *in situ*. The closer control is to the work place, the quicker are deviations from standards picked up; the time loss and possible production delay in getting samples approved is reduced, production and inspection personnel obtain a clearer idea of each other's responsibilities, and this should encourage teamwork. The strength of such arguments is lessened where delicate equipment and carefully-controlled testing conditions are important for measurement, such as in a standards room or where (because of noise, vibration, or dust) conditions are not suitable in the production setting. In the process industries, for instance, it is common to have control laboratories which are physically separate from the plant whose output they monitor. In special cases of expensive equipment or complex analysis, a larger undertaking may have group laboratories to which samples are sent for special tests to supplement the local control systems at factory level. Another interesting development is the use of outside testing or control facilities, such as those becoming increasingly available at industrial or national research establishments or at universities. In other situations, where the value of raw materials or bought-out components is high and their consistency is important, a company or government department may have its own resident inspectors at the suppliers' works.

It will be seen from our analysis that the planning and decision-making required to establish a quality-control system is quite a complex operation. A number of variables have to be considered and, naturally, their respective weight is a particular function of the technology and environment with which the company is associated. Nor can we presume that the relative merit of each variable remains unchanged over time. The planning of inspection systems is growing in importance as new plant, with greater rates of output, is often linked with higher accuracy in materials feeds and operation. Furthermore, to achieve higher standards of control, inspection equipment is becoming increasingly more sophisticated and expensive. In some areas of production automation has eliminated manual labour, and as a result drastically reduced direct labour costs. By comparison, in many cases inspection labour costs have not diminished proportionately, and consequently, inspection operations have attracted increasing management attention.

3 THE ORGANIZATION OF THE QUALITY-CONTROL FUNCTION

It is an important facet of a company's organization to determine the structure of its quality-control function. Essentially, this function has two main tasks:

a To provide specialist staff advice on quality determination and control to top management.

b To implement the company's control policies by the setting up of quality-control systems, and to maintain and improve these.

The emphasis on quality will, at times, conflict with financial and manufacturing aspects, and if the executive responsible for quality is subsidiary in position his voice will not get the appropriate attention. This will limit the standing of the quality-control function within the company, which, in turn, will have an effect on the calibre of its senior departmental staff. It is preferable that the executive responsible for quality is directly accountable to the manager or director in charge of manufacturing – a man who has overall responsibility and not just a quantitative production brief.

In a line and staff form of organization quality control is a staff function. In the overall business context it supports the basic manufacturing task. Its internal organization may, in turn, have its own line and staff structure, especially where the number of quality-control personnel is large. The detail structure is, of course, governed by a given company setting, but the typical example of a large light engineering inspection organization as shown in Fig. 10 provides an illustration of the possible range of activities.

In this particular illustration the line structure within the inspection function consists of the supplies and production-area superintendents and their subordinates. The planning, statistical, and specialist groups, etc, provide an internal staff service to the inspection function as a whole. In some cases the tool room and outside inspection groups are under the control of the production engineering or purchasing sections, respectively. While there may be arguments for this in practice, an integrated company approach to quality will be better served when one department is made responsible for all aspects of quality control. The structure of the department itself must, of course, be seen within the total framework of company organization, and the links with

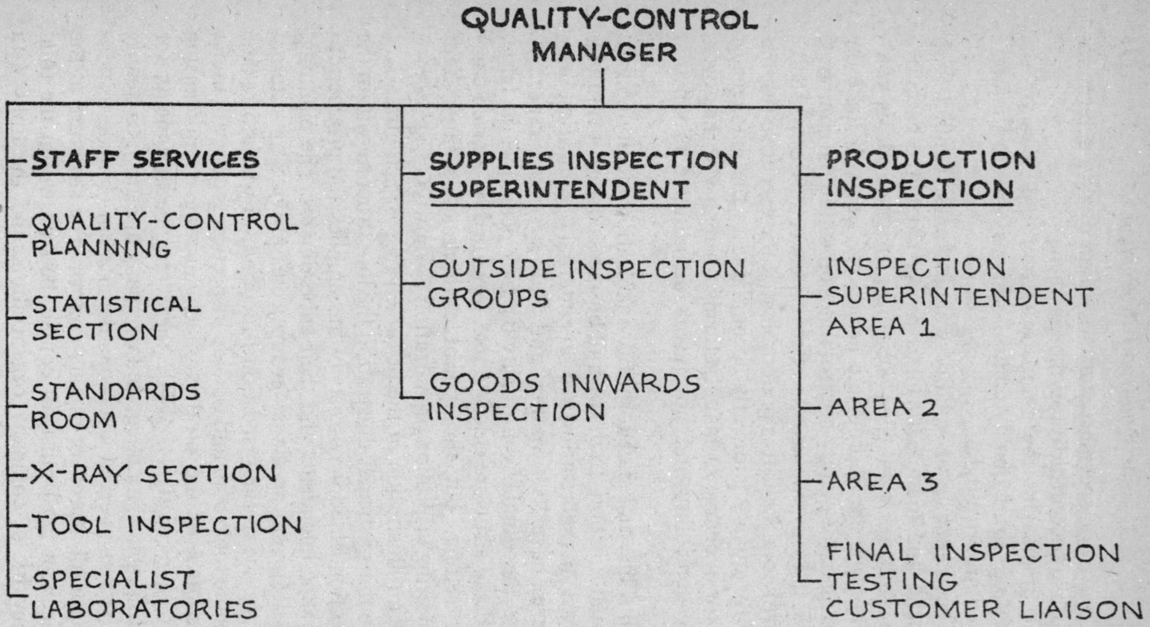

QUALITY-CONTROL MANAGER

STAFF SERVICES
- QUALITY-CONTROL PLANNING
- STATISTICAL SECTION
- STANDARDS ROOM
- X-RAY SECTION
- TOOL INSPECTION
- SPECIALIST LABORATORIES

SUPPLIES INSPECTION SUPERINTENDENT
- OUTSIDE INSPECTION GROUPS
- GOODS INWARDS INSPECTION

PRODUCTION INSPECTION
- INSPECTION SUPERINTENDENT AREA 1
- AREA 2
- AREA 3
- FINAL INSPECTION
- TESTING
- CUSTOMER LIAISON

Fig. 10 TYPICAL ORGANIZATION STRUCTURE – QUALITY-CONTROL DEPARTMENT – LARGE LIGHT ENGINEERING COMPANY

line management, particularly in production, should be visualized at the various levels.

4 THE NATURE OF QUALITY CONTROL

A number of quality-control systems exist which have their uses in a variety of settings, depending on the stringency of the control specification and its economics. A company may also, for instance, concentrate on one system, say, one based on statistical sampling techniques, but in special cases insist on 100 per cent inspection.

a Accept–reject inspection

This type of control involves a 100 per cent inspection of components and/or assembled products. Each item is measured or compared with a master unit, and if the deviation of the relevant property or dimension is beyond the limit set by the specification or drawing then the item is rejected. Where this type of control is required continuously and the quantities are substantial, it will be economic to 'tool up' for such inspection checks. 'Go and Not-go' or simple equivalent gauges will obviate measurement and reduce the inspection process to a minor manual operation and observation. In terms of man hours and labour costs such 100 per cent checks may, however, be expensive, but this might be justified where the product feature is critical or there has been previous difficulty in production or quality control. There is also the risk of human error with monotonous, repetitive inspection tasks. The simple accept–reject system, although very relevant if you quickly wish to segregate useful from useless components, gives little guide to the source of error, whether biased or random. It is in essence a filter system which may well avoid trouble in a given situation; but it cannot claim to be effective control because of the lack of detail feedback which permits corrective action to be taken.

b Selective assembly

Although selective assembly may be regarded as a special type of production task, it is appropriate to mention it here because it involves a 100 per cent inspection operation in respect of one or several product features. The classical case normally cited here is the matching of pistons and cylinders in car-engine assembly. Where very high tolerances cannot be guaranteed by a machine or they would involve disproportionate capital expenditure, it may be cheaper to widen the machining tolerance range, but within it, match the corresponding mating parts, so that finer tolerances in assembly are achieved. Thus slightly oversize pistons will be paired with slightly oversize cylinders. We have in fact an inspection and classification process. A number of acceptable categories are established, and selection is on such a category basis. Those parts which fall outside the overall acceptance range are rejected as before.

c **Sampling techniques**

The use of sampling techniques is widespread and statistical analysis is a well-known tool of quality control. In essence, sampling is possible, where the examination of a small quantity is a reliable guide to the characteristics of a large volume or number of parts. The effectiveness of sampling rests on the assumption that any batch is broadly homogeneous and that a sample chosen at random would yield a consistent pattern of properties. While the economics of sampling, as against full testing, are self-evident, there are also cases, such as with destructive testing, where sampling is the method by definition. It is important to choose an adequate and truly random sample, but once a minimum sample size for statistical analysis has been determined, the choice of larger samples, greater frequency, and higher accuracy is one of economics.

The sampling approach could reflect either of two basic techniques.

i Control by variables.

ii Control by attributes.

The 'control by variables' technique measures the spread of a sample in terms of its mean and standard deviation and then compares these with the acceptable standard value range. This technique is applicable where measurement and scale values can be used. In contrast, 'control by attribute' is in terms of a perceived, but not necessarily measured, feature, such as the smudging of a newly printed surface. An acceptable standard may allow a certain composite reject level, say, 0·2 per cent for defect A, 0·3 per cent for defect B, etc. If the number of faulty items in a given sample exceeds the permitted scale, then the sample is rejected. In the absence of measurement it is important to have clear definitions as to what constitutes a defect, as otherwise there is the risk of subjective assessments.

d **Control charts**

It is convenient, particularly with statistical analysis, to display sample data on a graphical basis by the use of suitably designed charts. Such charts are applicable both to control by variables and by attributes. The actual findings are plotted against a time scale which can be annotated by a plant or machine diary, such as '3 PM tools changed'. Furthermore, it will be possible to superimpose a corresponding distribution of a master batch and thus to highlight trends in the process under scrutiny. In this manner an early warning can be obtained, to signal when the performance, although still acceptable, approaches a control limit. For convenience of operation, particularly where plant adjustments take time to have the required effect, a central 'no action' zone may be defined on the chart, and this in turn is flanked by 'caution' and 'take correction' zones until the specification limits are reached. Once defined and developed, the charts can be compiled by relatively unskilled control personnel or automatically.

e **Plant capability studies**

In order to assess the nature of the quality-control system that can be applied to a given plant, it is important to have an initial and clear measure of the accuracy and limits of plant performance. This can be obtained by carefully controlled, supervised, and recorded trial runs, Such performance, under 'optimum' conditions, will then be analysed and the spread of data evaluated. From this it will be possible to assess whether the nature of the process variations is such that the plant is capable of working to specified limits or not and, if not, what modifications may be needed to achieve the desired improvement. It will also be possible to determine whether the plant is amenable to statistical control or whether 100 per cent inspection is required.

Similar information about plant capabilities may be derived from past control charts, but as these reflect production 'history' they may not really give sufficient guidance on capability, unless such a history contains a certain amount of plant investigation.

5 OPERATOR INSPECTION

So far the presumption has been that inspection work and quality control is the sole province of an inspection department. While such a department may plan and determine appropriate quality-control levels, in a number of industries some of the routine inspection work is, in fact, delegated to production labour. This is especially the case where the work is responsible by nature and where the work cycle lends itself conveniently to operator checks. In such cases it is more economical for a section inspector to supplement rather than to duplicate the checks which have already been included or implied in the operator's routine. This trend towards operator inspection may further develop as plant operation becomes more a matter of attendant supervision rather than a set of physical tasks.

In some fields of production, such as in certain sections of the shoe industry where there is still room for some craft pride and skill, it may be part of the management philosophy to appeal to the pride and integrity of workers to maintain their own control of quality. The human relationships between inspector and production worker are not normally of the easiest kind. The implied judgement when work is sent back for rectification or rejected altogether affects the atmosphere on the shop floor and the motivation of workpeople. The difficulties are frequently accentuated when production departments are either on piece work or some other form of incentive scheme primarily governed by output figures. Where management persuasion succeeds, there may be the tangible savings of reduced inspection staff. The intangible benefits, such as a more responsible work and quality attitude, are by no mean negligible and may, in turn, improve the tone of labour relations within a plant. Systems which harness the operator's latent desire for higher-quality work and his expert detailed knowledge of certain production operations are known as Zero Defects Programmes. It should be stressed that such systems do not release management from its basic responsibility for product quality, but they help it to achieve such a commitment – by participation.

There are a number of production applications in the light engineering field and with flow-process operations, such as in glass-bottle manufacture, where the bulk of the labour costs on a production line are incurred on examination and sorting. The first type of situation may reflect an interim stage in process development where the plant is automatic but not yet sufficiently consistent to be entirely trusted. The manual labour, originally superseded by the new plant, is put on 100 per cent inspection work, but as in most such cases the plant output has increased, unit labour costs are still reduced. In the other situation, where quality control is usually by attribute, no foolproof automatic sorting device is as yet available on an economic basis.

Again, on aircraft and associated eleetronic work, where quality control and reliability testing is critical, the man hours spent on quality and reliability assurance can substantially exceed the actual time required for production and assembly. The distinction here between assembly and inspection work may also be somewhat blurred because the technician employed on systems assembly may be responsible for much of the fault-finding work.

It can be seen, from these examples, that the actual

routine work division between the production and quality-control functions is by no means always clear. With a wide variety of production processes, involving a great range of skills and labour requirements, it is difficult to be dogmatic as to who does a particular inspection task. On the other hand, there is no doubt about the administrative division between those responsible for quality and those concerned with the achievement of a set production programme. Although specific and separate in organization, these two functions have to be skilled in the integration of their respective contributions so as to achieve effective and economic manufacture. It is a management task to ensure that such working integration exists.

6   AUTOMATION AND QUALITY CONTROL

Two separate aspects can be considered under this heading. Firstly, the impact of plant automation on quality-control methods and systems, and secondly, the automation of certain inspection methods, irrespective of the plant to which they are applied. The first aspect is better known as the impact of automation has transcended the specialist departmental level, but the significance of the second is growing, even where process plant conditions remain unaltered.

The general effect of plant automation on quality control has been similar to that on production. Many, if not all, of the routine monitoring tasks have been taken over by automatic control, and the closed loop of feedback data and control signal – when production conditions vary – is analogous to the inspector/operator relationship. Provided a suitable alarm signal is given, or the plant shuts itself down when the specification limits are exceeded, quality-control efforts can be concentrated on improvement rather than be confined to general plant supervision. The records that can be made available by an automatic or computer-controlled plant represent extensive control data on which further quality-development work can be based. This does not mean that routine checks need never be carried out, but the emphasis of quality control is no longer in that direction. A parallel pattern is also developing with numerically controlled machine tools, which have their own built-in control systems, and here, too, the amount of inspection work that would have been required with equivalent conventional plant has been substantially reduced.

Inspection equipment itself has developed along similar lines to production plant; it has generally become more accurate, sophisticated, and expensive. There have, however, been a number of successful, simple, and relatively cheap applications of new scientific developments, especially in the field of photo-electric and electronic scanning. There has also been a corresponding increase in the variety of inspection equipment, much of which has been designed by the users to handle specific quality problems. Such developments have been prompted, and automatic inspection devices generally encouraged, where there is a need for 100 per cent inspection on an accept–reject basis. In an integrated production line, whether it is automatic or not, automatic inspection equipment can be incorporated as a separate work station; and it is normal for such equipment not only to appraise the defect specified but also to deflect such a faulty item to a separate chute or conveyor. A similar development is the incorporation of such an automatic inspection device into a machine, and the automatic quality check then becomes the final element of a particular set of operations.

Where automation is feasible and economic in quality control, it generally reduces the amount of routine inspection. It also simplifies the more complex inspection tasks by automatic measuring and recording, digital read-outs, and print-outs. It has lessened the 'organizational distance' between the laboratory and the shop floor by introducing to the latter sensitive and delicate control equipment which hitherto was thought more suitable for the laboratory. As with production, the long-term trend favours the specialist technologist, who will be concerned more with the engineering, planning, and systems design of quality control rather than the maintenance of routine systems of inspection.

7 THE APPLICATION OF QUALITY-CONTROL EXPERIENCE

While the basic purpose of the quality-control function is to determine and to maintain quality levels, an experienced quality-control section can exert a wider influence within a manufacturing organization than its strict terms of reference might suggest. For instance, the development of appropriate quantity and quality tolerances, inspection and sampling clauses in contractual negotiation involves the quality-control department. There may be occasional bargains, such as with the purchase of raw materials which may be sub-standard for their original purpose but are still suitable for alternative applications. Without the guidance from its quality-control department, a business may be at undue risk when considering such commercial opportunities. In fact, with tight quality control the firm can make substantial savings where otherwise a higher grade of material would have to be bought in order to 'play safe'. At the other end of the scale a good quality-control system helps a company when pressed by a customer who wants to pass back the losses of an ill-considered product application. Again, inspection advice can be useful in machine specification and design; properly maintained quality records constitute here factual arguments.

Experience and success in quality control can be harnessed, and effective production management will ensure that the contribution of the quality-control department is put to the fullest and widest use.

REFERENCES

1 D. S. Davies, and M. C. McCarthy: *Introduction to Technological Economics*, Wiley, 1967.

FURTHER READING

L. F. Thomas: *The Control of Quality*, Thames and Hudson, 1965.

H. Rissick: *Quality Control in Production*, Pitman, 1947.

A. F. Cowan: *Quality Control for the Manager*, Pergamon, 1964.

CHAPTER SIX

Plant Engineering and Services

Whereas the planning engineer or the production technologist is primarily concerned with the specification and
introduction of working methods and production plant, as
described in Chapter Three, the plant or works engineer
and his department provide those basic services which
keep the installed plant in operation. To achieve such an
object, the plant engineer is concerned with aspects of plant
layout, maintenance, safety, building, and plant services.
In a large factory his department may be substantial and
his precise title may reflect senior management status. In
many process plants his labour force is bigger than that on
production.

The organizational setting of the plant department may
be visualized from Fig. 11. It is normal for the plant engineer
or manager to be directly responsible to the works manager.

The precise relationships between the plant engineer/
manager and his colleagues are very much a function of the
company and the technological processes it employs. In the
process and allied industries, such as power generation,
which essentially work 'around the clock' the plant
engineer's role is enhanced because of the strong pressure to
maintain continuity of production. The extent of the plant
manager's command can be shown by a typical organization chart relating to the plant-engineering function in an
oil refinery or large chemical works (see Fig. 12).

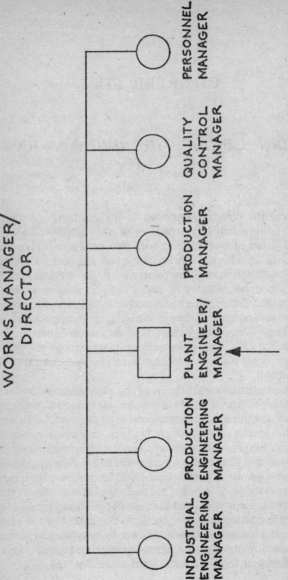

Fig. 11 THE PLANT ENGINEER/MANAGER AND HIS MAIN WORKS COLLEAGUES AT THE SAME LEVEL OF AUTHORITY (TYPICAL MEDIUM/LARGE ENGINEERING COMPANY)

1   THE ROLE OF PLANT MAINTENANCE

The engineering maintenance of production plant is regarded by most managers as a necessary evil. The costs of labour, spare parts, and plant down time can be substantial, and the only reason why such expenditures are incurred is that the alternative costs in terms of plant failure, emergency work, and safety hazards can be even worse. The temptation to run production plants non-stop without adequate maintenance may be there, and can even be sometimes justified financially when a special non-recurring opportunity presents itself or the plant may be obsolescent in the near future, anyway. But the case for effective plant maintenance is strong in so far as it helps to ensure the continuity of a production unit. This is quite apart from any requirements covered by the Factories Act 1961 or associated regulations. Neither would the complete neglect of maintenance help the tone of industrial relations, especially where processes may have latent hazards.

a   **The purpose of maintenance**

Plant maintenance is essentially a service to production. It is not normally regarded as a basic business activity, but without it one of the three basic business functions – manufacture – would before long cease as an economic activity. While the precise purposes of plant maintenance may differ with various companies, the following are usually regarded as the most important objectives:

1   To keep production plant in a condition that will permit the attainment of its design specification. This emphasis on the achievement of the design function is important; just to keep plant running is insufficient, if this means that the output is found wanting, both in quality and quantity. If a substantial capital investment is reflected in the purchase of new plant this is normally justified in terms of 'net benefit' (the total, resulting, discounted net cash flow over the projected life of the equipment). If such net benefit does not materialize because a basic presumption in an investment evaluation – the presumption

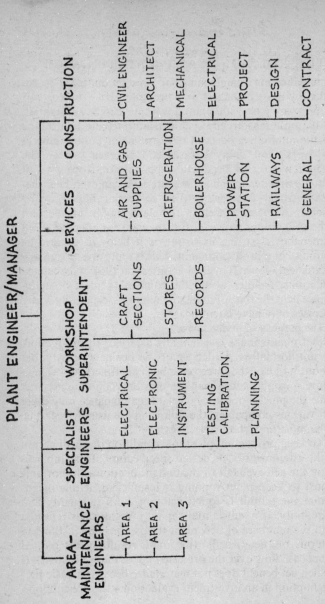

Fig. 12 TYPICAL ORGANIZATION CHART OF THE PLANT ENGINEERING FUNCTION IN A

of design-performance achievement – is not being met in practice because of lack or inadequacy of maintenance, then this could have serious financial repercussions.

2 To keep unit production costs to a minimum. A production unit may achieve its performance specification, but in doing so requires more man hours or materials. This will, of course, also affect the economics of its operation. For instance, lack of effective maintenance may lead to extra machine-tool setting time at the start of a production run. Also, the resulting excess wear may cause early slackness of machine slides, and extra time or effort will be needed to ensure the accuracy of machined components.

3 Consistent with objectives No 1 and 2, to keep actual maintenance costs to a minimum. Inadequate maintenance, leading to plant failure, where the resulting emergency causes heavy direct and consequential costs, may in the end be more expensive than consistent and regular preventive maintenance. Where adequate records are kept, a plant department can plan routines on the basis of production or time cycles that cut the overall maintenance costs to a minimum. Such reduction of maintenance expenditure must, of course, have no undue repercussions on direct production costs. To save £1,000 per annum on maintenance, which adds £2,000 per annum to direct production costs – or for that matter, the other way round – would be ludicrous. It does occur, however, where there is no proper costing or budgetary control, and, even with appropriate control systems, it can happen if there is no integrated, overall scrutiny of departmental costs.

4 To improve general working conditions and plant operations. This is the general task of good factory housekeeping. This includes the maintenance and painting of the building fabric, service piping, the cleaning of roof lights, and all those many tasks which, individually, seem petty but in sum total make a working area

wholesome. This also covers the avoidance of nuisances, dust, dirt, etc, and the maintenance of heating and ventilating installations.

b **Criteria for maintenance policies**

While the purposes of plant maintenance seem self-evident and there is the temptation to leave it all to the plant department, provided its budgets are not excessive, there is much to be said for the development of coherent maintenance policies. Such policies should emanate from the highest works management level and be based on advice from the plant and production departments. Overall direction is necessary here: to leave maintenance plans and their integration with the total manufacturing situation to a partial departmental view would be the negation of management. For instance, the relining of a blast furnace or a glass-producing furnace may be such a major task in terms of cost and loss of output that the maintenance of such equipment becomes a matter for board attention. The development of maintenance policies has specific aspects for most companies, but the following criteria may be relevant when it comes to their formulation:

1 The performance and the nature of construction of the plant involved. For instance, if performance requirements are exacting and the 'design margin' of the equipment is modest, then careful maintenance may be imperative. In more routine applications stringent maintenance requirements may not be quite so critical.

2 The nature of the machine environment. Where plant has to operate in dusty, abrasive, hot, or acidic conditions, this will affect maintenance needs.

3 The manner of plant grouping. Where equipment operates in discrete units, the failure of one item of equipment, while possibly an emergency in its own right, is not quite so critical compared to a parallel situation where such unit is an integral part of a flow line and possibly causes the stoppage of all other equipment on that line as well.

4 Hazards and safety requirements. Where a process is

hazardous and contact with, or exposure to, process materials is dangerous, then a high standard of maintenance is imperative.

5 The characteristics of maintenance operations. If these involve substantial dislocation and costs, such as with furnace relining, then the approach to maintenance will be different from the setting where most of the equipment can be overhauled or replaced within a day, whenever this suits production.

6 The nature of anticipated plant failure. The first aspect here is the risk and the likely frequency of such an event. Past records can provide useful case histories and background data. The character of failure is also important; whether it is likely to be confined largely to one group of items, such as bearings or seals, or whether it could stem from a wide variety of causes. The third aspect reflects the possible consequences of a failure. Aircraft maintenance, for instance, is stringent by industrial standards because minor failures may cause major disasters. Similarly, if a plant breakdown could cause explosions, fire, or radiation hazards it will be considered in quite a different light to the failure where a machine just stops. The accessibility of the plant and the ease of repair are naturally relevant to this aspect.

The various criteria may lead to composite maintenance policies. But if all major aspects are thus taken into account the terms of reference within which maintenance work can then be planned and organized will provide correspondingly better guidance.

c **Types of maintenance work**

Within the framework of established maintenance policies, it will now be possible to set up a system of maintenance that can make its contribution to the effectiveness of the production plant. Such a maintenance system can conveniently be broken into the following broad classification:

1 *Daily routine inspection and servicing.* This may include lubrication, the checking of guards or safety devices,

inspection of belt drives, etc. Such tasks may be carried out at a convenient moment of stoppage, such as during the lunch break, or, where planned accordingly, while the plant is in continuous operation.

2 *Scheduled maintenance.* This provides for more extensive inspection and, possibly, for the stripping down of key assemblies and replacement of parts. The frequency and nature of such work depends on the rate of wear in operation, and this may be determined in the light of experience as compiled from plant records. The work may either be carried out *in situ* or in the plant workshops. The timing of scheduled maintenance may be either governed by the ability of manufacturing departments to release the equipment from production work or by planned plant shutdowns incorporated in the overall production programme, which may be preferable in the long run. Scheduled maintenance facilitates the forward planning of specific overhaul tasks and the more effective use of maintenance labour.

3 *Preventive maintenance.* This is a development of scheduled maintenance which has the object of eliminating breakdowns altogether. As such, it involves the detailed development of inspection procedures, plant overhauls, and part or equipment replacements, even if there is at times still useful life in some of the components replaced. It also allows for the incorporation of modifications and improvements which not only increase plant reliability but also bring the plant up to date. Preventive maintenance requires complete and detailed planning. It can be expensive in overhaul work and may put equipment out of action for weeks or, possibly, months. The plant may be overhauled in the company's workshops or might have to be sent out to specialist contractors. But such expense and attention may be justified in those cases where the cost of plant breakdown is serious or where otherwise there would be undue hazards to operating personnel.

4 *Outside contract maintenance.* There is a growing

tendency for specialist equipment, such as weighing machines, instruments, electronic equipment, etc, to be maintained by the supplier on a contract basis. This is particularly so where there would otherwise be a risk of statutory infringement, such as of the Weights and Measures Acts, which may require the maintenance of the equipment concerned by 'competent' persons. There is, of course, the wider problem that most of the smaller and many of the medium-sized businesses do not have the required range of technical skill in their plant department for such specialist and often technologically advanced equipment.

5 *Breakdown maintenance.* Such an approach to maintenance anticipates equipment to continue in production until it fails. When failure occurs, the whole weight of the maintenance facilities is thrown into the emergency until the defective plant resumes production. Such an approach may seem unsystematic and careless, but there can be situations where it is justifiable. The smaller workshop, with standard equipment applied to not very arduous tasks, and a production supervision experienced with the type of plant in use, may find that its annual maintenance labour costs may be lower in such cases, despite the heavy overtime commitments that may occasionally be incurred. Also, if machine utilization is not too concentrated and a given production job can be put on a number of alternative machines, there may not be too heavy a price in terms of loss of output. Essentially, such an approach reflects the assessment of risk and the dislocation a plant failure may cause.

d **Aspects of maintenance management**

Plant maintenance commitments are not quite as predictable as routine production tasks because of the risk of some unforeseen mishap or failure, which even the most sophisticated preventive maintenance system cannot always eliminate. Nevertheless, it will be possible and necessary to establish cost budgets for plant maintenance activities. A sensible establishment figure for maintenance labour presupposes some work measurement or analytical estimating, and although it may not always be practical to go into great detail, work-study methods can find useful application here. Some measure of work and cost is better than nothing at all, and even if some variances or excess costs are galling, such deviations, when appropriately highlighted, bring maintenance work to the attention of a responsible management.

While possibly irksome and time consuming, the keeping of suitable plant records will simplify and save maintenance work. The company plant register may form the basis of such records which furnish the 'life experience' of an operating plant. Contained in such a record will be the details, costs and dates of repairs, overhauls and modifications, causes of failure, and, where helpful, results of tests or commissioning runs. Such information will permit prediction about the likely behaviour of the plant in operation and provide guidance on the planning of maintenance work, the provision of spares, and, possibly, methods of operation.

The administration of maintenance work and its relationships with the various production departments is of some importance. For instance, requests to carry out certain maintenance tasks should come on a standard document, in line with clearly defined practice, and should be raised by a responsible section manager in production. It is the responsibility of production management, after consultation with the plant department, to ensure that production plant is kept in a reasonable working condition and to make arrangements accordingly. Upon the receipt of the appropriate requests, the plant department issues detail job instructions, prepares estimates and work programmes, and after consultation with production and due budget sanction it carries out the work. Costs and man hours are entered on a job sheet against the job number issued, and the total expenditure will in due course be debited against the production unit concerned. Wherever costs can be apportioned with reasonable accuracy – and this should be the majority of cases – it is desirable that a production department is first supplied with an estimate and then charged with such work;

otherwise there is no prospect of effective cost control of maintenance tasks.

Finally, two wider aspects of plant management require consideration. Firstly, there is the possible installation of standby plant in those cases where it is vital to have continuous operation. This often happens with process plants throughout which, for instance, cooling water must circulate and duplicate pumps are installed. The availability of two pumps makes it more certain that one is always on stream or, alternatively, the basic duty can be spread over two pumps and a third can be put in as a standby unit. A decision on standby equipment relates the additional capital costs against the benefits of more continuous operation of a large production plant. It also facilitates maintenance work, as one unit is spare at any given moment. Secondly, there is the general question of maintenance spares. How much should a company hold? The more comprehensive its spares inventory, the better will it be able to handle emergency repairs. But its investment in stores and its carrying charges will be correspondingly heavier. There is also the risk of physical deterioration and the obsolescence of such parts. A plant engineer may well find that with each item of equipment the optimum spares level is different. Much depends here on past equipment experience and the supplier's reputation for service. It is fairly common to ask suppliers to furnish recommended spares with their main plant delivery, because they are often cheaper and supplied more quickly when made up as part of a main order. It is also useful to have such spares available for possible trouble on commissioning runs.

2 PLANT REPLACEMENT

Despite continuous maintenance attention, overhauls, and modifications, there will be a gradual deterioration in the state of production plant. This will show itself in a number of ways which may be either quantitative, in terms of output or efficiency, or qualitative, in terms of product characteristics. With deterioration, it will take increasingly more maintenance to keep output to specification until the stage is reached when a machine will no longer meet its tasks or to maintain it for such a purpose becomes too costly. The precise rate of deterioration is, of course, also affected by

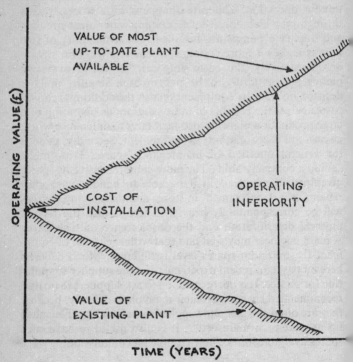

Fig. 13 CONCEPT OF 'OPERATING INFERIORITY'

skill in operation and the care taken in maintenance. But whatever its rate, there will come a time when a replacement decision needs to be made.

With the passage of time it also becomes less likely that a given piece of equipment will be replaced by an identical unit, even if such a unit is still available. Technical change affects what the supplier has to offer and what the user requires. The replacement decision is as much affected by new plant developments as by the deterioration of existing equipment. Without even taking the example of rapid obsolescence, there are many fields of production where the comparative new equipment is superior in terms of output, quality, or unit operating costs. As time passes, the existing plant acquires what Terborgh[1] describes as a growing 'operating inferiority'. This consists of: (a) the loss in operating value of the existing plant due to deterioration, and (b) the growing value of new equipment available to the company and its competitors, which incorporates more advanced techniques.

A parallel development, in most cases, is also the greater capital cost of replacement plant, even if the effects of inflation are taken into account.

A machine is displaced when it is deleted from its designated manufacturing task, ie, the task for which it was originally acquired. For instance, a tool-room jig borer may, after extended use, be able to work only to accuracies of ± 0.002 in., whereas the work requires accuracies of ± 0.0005 in. It does not follow that the machine will consequently be disposed of as scrap; it can be given less exacting secondary or tertiary tasks as its usefulness diminishes. Such a process of 'functional degradation' depends, of course, on the opportunities within a factory for the use of equipment which has been displaced from its original role. The machine can, of course, be sold as a working unit in the second-hand market, if one exists.

a **The nature of the replacement plant**

The equipment which takes over the vacant role will in most cases come from outside, but need not necessarily be always new. Such equipment is termed a primary replacement. Where the replacement is already owned by the company which has transferred it from some other use, then this is known as secondary replacement. While there is little published data on this secondary type of replacement, there is, in practice, considerable transfer of standard equipment within manufacturing groups, from one factory to another.

The replacement plant may be quite different in principle or construction and yet perform a similar duty, such as when a rotary air compressor replaces a reciprocating unit. More often the replacement equipment is similar, but may have a number of refinements or additional controls. The opportunity can also be taken, as part of the replacement decision, to increase plant capacity by introducing equipment which works at a faster rate or has a number of parallel operating streams, instead of one. Such changes may, in turn, involve a certain amount of operator training and adjustments in manning, maintenance, or inspection routines. A work section that may have standardized certain types of production equipment some years earlier may no longer be able to do so. For a while it is between two 'machine generations', so to speak.

b **The timing of replacement decisions**

The engineer is attracted by the prospect of new plant; the businessman is often frightened by it. The timing of plant replacements requires some judgement, but it is not normally a matter here of a once-for-all opportunity. The choice is usually between replacement now or its deferment for one or more years. The benefits that may actuate a particular replacement decision may not, however, remain constant. For example, there may be temporary and non-recurring marketing opportunities (these can be taken, by having a replacement overlap period, giving a short-term peak capacity). Alternatively, there may, for a while, be a competitive advantage in the use of improved and cheaper working methods. There is also the converse fear that buying a new plant invites extra risks of early obsolescence when there is an anticipation of more fundamental changes. Then, of course, there is the effect of taxation, whether actual or impending, depreciation allowances, and investment grants. When the operating inferiority of the existing equipment is such, in terms of costs of production or rate of value produced, that the investment in replacement plant can be justified in terms of incremental and realizable benefits, then it will be worth while to replace. Such an investment calculation will, of course, have to take into account the relative performances, as already established, and such future trends as may affect the relative operating economics of the plants concerned.

Extending from this, successful plant-replacement planning then becomes a matter of keeping both the combined operating inferiority and the necessary capital expenditure to a minimum, ie, to keep the production plant as up to date as possible, consistent with minimum plant investment. It will be noted that the original investment outlay on the existing plant, the 'sunk cost', is irrelevant to the replacement decision. To write off plant that has still a considerable book value may be a painful exercise, but a replacement decision does not necessarily improve with the disturbing influence of a past miscalculation.

c **Making the replacement decision**

The determination of when and how a plant should be replaced is an interdepartmental process, as a number of aspects are usually involved. Depending on the type of equipment involved, it will become either a part of the production-planning function, or the plant engineer will be charged with the staff work to prepare a suitable case for the replacement. He will collate such relevant information as may be available from other departments, particularly cost data in respect of the existing equipment and its proposed replacement. It will remain the responsibility of works management to interpret relevant company policy and the general implications of the proposal, and for the board of the company to authorize the proposed expenditure, if this exceeds the limits within which the various levels of management can use their discretion.

3 PLANT SERVICES

No production plant can operate effectively without the provision of supporting services. These include the supply of electric power, steam, hot or cold water, refrigerants, compressed or purified air, gases, etc. In some engineering shops there may only be need for electric power and compressed air, but in many process units the number of different services, and the quantities required, may be much greater. There is also the provision of allied facilities, such as material-handling equipment (where this is not integrated with production plant), internal transport, and effluent disposal. As Fig. 12 suggests, the plant facilities provided to support production can be extensive in large factories and, although behind the scenes and therefore not always appreciated by production personnel, they can call for substantial investment, manpower, and organization. In a book primarily concerned with the organization of production there is room only for a brief reference to such broad and mainly technical areas. Nevertheless, an awareness of these services, their problems, costs, and general use of company resources makes for sounder judgement in the direction of manufacturing activities.

a **Electric power**

In many ways this is the most convenient type of power supply because of its inherent cleanliness and flexibility in application. While it is normal for a factory to take the bulk of its requirements from the local electricity board, there are quite a number of manufacturing units which generate a substantial portion of their own needs. This happens usually when a process requires large quantities of low-pressure steam and, as the economics of steam raising favour high-pressure systems, the excess pressure can be used for electric-power generation. A factory could also have surpluses of electric power which it could sell back to the 'supplying' authorities. While the negotiation of supplies for general factory use is an aspect of construction and plant engineering, production management is still concerned with it: most manufacturing activities lead to long-term increases in power consumed, corresponding to the growth in production, even if the power needed per unit output declines. The greater the power requirement, the more economic will it be in cabling and equipment to take supplies at a high voltage, say, 11,000 volts, instead of 415/440 volts, which is normal for small industrial users. A good balance of usage in terms of current taken (power factor) and the distribution of peak loads will avoid the risk of contract penalties and otherwise make for economy. As electric-power costs for a sizeable process plant can exceed £500,000 per annum, and in some cases are the highest individual processing costs, this aspect deserves attention.

In the planning of individual working areas provision is desirable for additional power outlets on departmental distribution boards, even if the floor space looks fully taken up by production plant. Where equipment is arranged on flow-line principles and its layout may be modified when there are product or model changes, then the provision of convenient and flexible power connexions, usually from above, deserves consideration, even if the capital cost of such a flexible supply system is relatively high.

Needless to say, the plant engineer and production management have a specific responsibility as to the safety of equipment and correct working practices, as far as anything electrical is concerned.

b Steam supplies

Where a manufacturing unit requires steam for process use, it is the normal practice to have a boiler plant. While a boiler house with its chimney used to be a feature of the industrial landscape, modern boiler plant is relatively compact for its capacity, and in many new factories, with modest steam usage, the boiler house is little more than an annexe to the manufacturing areas. Nevertheless, it does usually remain separated by partition or wall, to avoid interference with production, particularly in terms of dust or heat, and at times, significantly, to keep various labour grades apart. While boilers may be either oil- or coal- fired, the present trend is towards oil, mainly on the grounds of costs, cleanliness, and convenient storage. From commercial and planning aspects, forward bulk contracts are important, while the convenience and regularity of fuel supply determine the minimum fuel stock levels to be held by the factory to avoid production shut-downs. The nature of water usage and treatment, condensate collection, etc, although more technical and specialized topics, have, nevertheless, significant cost implications. The actual boiler units require specific statutory and insurance inspections, and where a continuous process load exists, most users prefer a standby plant to allow for such inspections and maintenance. Industrial boilers are sized in terms of steam-raising capacity, ie, the amount of steam raised per hour of operation, and the stop-valve pressure of the steam as it leaves the boiler. It is part of the process-engineering and production-planning task to specify each individual steam-usage requirement, in terms of pressure and quantity, and to establish, if necessary, the diversity of the steam-usage pattern for overall load evaluation and boiler sizing. A good deal of ancillary equipment, such as pumps, fan units, deaerators, etc, may be installed, and modern boiler controls are such that most load patterns can be handled automatically. Very little, if any, operator attendance is now necessary for some of the most recent oil-fired 'package-unit' types of boiler.

The steam distribution piping, its isolating and control valves, and other constituents, such as strainers, traps, etc, require appropriate heat insulation and maintenance. Where the plant and office heating load is considerable, calorifiers may be used, as a means of heat exchange, to transfer heat from the factory steam circuit to the domestic type of radiator systems.

c Compressed air

This is a general utility in most factories which is installed as an automatic system, and as, on the whole, it provides trouble-free service, it is usually taken for granted. It becomes significant in a process sense only when the air has to have a high purity or dryness standard, has to be sterile or oil free. Such more exacting requirements apply largely to instrument air systems on automatic process plant, where moisture deposition and corrosion could cause instrument or control failure, and thus constitute an operating hazard. Similarly, where the air actually enters a process stream, impurities may have undesirable side effects or reduce the yield of chemical reactions. For general engineering and work use, compressed air has a wide application to the following:

1 Machine Operation. Air-operated clamps, chucks, and other work-holding devices are in common use.
2 Individual Machine Controls. This covers the whole range of pneumatic machine controls and interlocks which are served from the factory supply.
3 Machine Power. Applications here include air-driven drills and cutting equipment, particularly where there is a flame hazard and conventional electrical equipment constitutes a risk.
4 Mechanical Handling. This includes a whole range of techniques, from the fluidizing of powders in ducting to high-pressure air blasts which place or remove work from conveyor belts.

Compressor installations are normally sized in terms of the free volume of air taken into the system and the output delivery pressure. Depending on this, the actual compressors may be reciprocating, 'V' type or rotary units. An electric drive is most common, and this could be either directly coupled or, with the larger type of unit, be through belt transmission. It is normal practice to provide an aftercooler to eliminate most of the moisture that would otherwise settle out when the high-pressure air cools in the distribution system or at the point of use. An air receiver usually serves as an intermediate air-storage unit to allow for a variable usage pattern and to reduce pressure pulsations. As high-pressure air is potentially hazardous, statutory inspection and maintenance requirements have to be met. The actual air-distribution system is essentially a matter for plant engineering, but from a production point of view the flexibility of supply points, the range of pressures available, and ease of extension may be of some importance.

d Cooling facilities

These fall primarily into two divisions:

1 Refrigeration.
2 The provision of cooling water.

The general application of refrigeration to manufacturing processes has grown in recent years, although it has long been commonplace in some process industries. Varied applications occur in food manufacture, chemical processing, plastic moulding, etc. There is usually scope for a refrigeration application where a heat input, which is part of a production process, has to be removed quickly after the completion of the desired operation. The use of refrigeration for storage purposes is, of course, common knowledge.

Refrigeration concerns itself with the cooling of materials from ambient temperature to about minus 150° C, but the greater number of commercial installations are unlikely to operate much below temperatures of about minus 30° C. Most of the larger industrial units work on the vapour-compression system which essentially involves a compressor, condenser, liquid refrigerant storage, an expansion valve, and the process area from which the heat is extracted to achieve the desired cooling effect. Where the risk of refrigerant leakage and contamination could be serious, as with food storage, the system normally cools a brine circuit, which in turn abstracts heat from the storage area. Refrigeration plants are sized in terms of 'tons of refrigeration', which is a measure of heat absorption per hour. Below the fifty-ton size, most of the plants are package units on a common bedplate, ready for connecting up. Above such size and for the more specialized duties they are mostly designed to the user's specification. While the plant can usually operate automatically upon satisfactory commissioning, maintenance is important. In some chemical processes the refrigeration unit may be integral with the process plant, but in most cases it is segregated from production, particularly if there is the nuisance of smell, from ammonia, or vibration. Refrigerant distribution is important; cold insulation and low-temperature fittings are proportionately more costly, and the heat gain outside the process area must be kept within reasonable limits.

The least expensive way of providing cooling water is to pump it from a nearby river or canal and to return it after use. Unfortunately the rate of industrial usage is now so heavy that river boards, with other amenities in mind, are often unable or unwilling to permit the rate of water extraction required for production processes. Sea water is also used where large cooling loads are involved, but extra precautions have to be taken here against marine corrosion. Where no large-scale cooling-water supply is available, a factory will have to recirculate its own cooling water and keep its temperature down with the use of cooling towers. These may be the natural-draught type, the large curved concrete structures which figure so prominently near inland power stations, or the smaller induced or forced-draught units, where the cooling air flow is handled by large fans. The latter types may be more convenient to the compact factory because of space requirements. In terms of distribution, piping, supply points, and pumps, cooling-water systems can be a substantial investment; and where production processes depend on them, maintenance here will be just as important as for any other piece of production plant.

e **Air conditioning**

Recently a technical journal, when describing the microcircuit production line of a well-known electronic company, carried the following headline: 'A Speck of Dust Means a Reject'. The article gave an account of the production environment in which these circuits were made. Air temperature was kept between 72° and 74° F, the air was cleaned to remove dust particles as small as 0·5 micron (1 micron = 0·001 millimetre) in size, there were 50–55 air changes each hour, and humidity was controlled at 50 and 25 per cent respectively. To achieve such controlled conditions over a sizeable area may require considerable heating or cooling loads, depending on the time, day, and seasonal variations. This, in turn, may call for substantial heating and refrigeration units, dehumidifiers, filtration equipment, etc, all integrated within an automatic-control system. The production area has to be sealed off and insulated, it has to be provided with airlocks through which all access is routed, all dust-producing surfaces have to be removed or covered. Operators have to be supplied with special clothes, strict working routines have to be established, and the production area begins to look like a hospital operating theatre. This trend towards a more exacting control of the production environment, due to higher reliability requirements and component miniaturization, has increased the work of the plant department. Although conditions may not necessarily be as onerous in other situations, the growth of heating and ventilating, which is designed for a higher standard of human comfort rather than process needs, has also given a fillip to a new technology which will be increasingly important to production.

4 PLANT LAYOUT ASPECTS

The relevance of layout studies to production planning has already been described in Chapter Three. While pure production aspects are important, they are not the only ones to be considered within the total manufacturing context. The argument for a particular production layout is a function of the volume of output it will handle. Thus in a mass-production unit the savings in production time and costs, though marginal per unit produced, become so telling because of quantity that most other considerations are dwarfed. This will not be the case necessarily with a jobbing shop or small batch production.

a Types of plant layout

Depending on the overall manufacturing and business situation, four basic types of plant layout can be distinguished.

i Random layout. This may be the layout of a small jobbing unit or a small, new, owner-managed factory.

Its scale is so small that no distance is critical. The element of personal supervision, particularly in the latter case, is stronger, and the emphasis on flexibility does not encourage too heavy a commitment to a particular layout pattern. While obvious cases of incompatibility between adjacent plant items are avoided on technical grounds, the layout in terms of plant is mixed. In essence, it reflects the organic growth of a small manufacturing organization.

ii *Grouped layout.*   This is commonplace in many medium engineering plants. In substance, the manufacturing layout is composed of a number of specialist sections, each geographically self-contained, such as a press shop, heat treatment, gear cutting, milling, or turret lathe sections, etc. Each section carries out its appropriate work, irrespective of the final product destination or assembly point. The advantages of such a layout consist of easier work supervision, economy in specialist plant services, where required, and the confinement of nuisances, etc, to limited areas. Against this, the lines of travel for work in progress may be longer, and it might be difficult at times to locate small lot jobs. Such grouping is largely a compromise, and there are cases where the original balance of arguments has since disappeared but the benefits of rearrangement do not justify the dislocation involved.

iii *Flow production layout.*   This type of layout physically follows the flow-process chart and finds particular expression in the arrangement of assembly and feeder lines on mass production. Everything is arranged to limit operator movement and to reduce the distance the work has to travel. There may be a considerable variety of equipment lined up alongside each other, but whatever disadvantages this might possibly have from a services or maintenance point of view will be subordinate to achieving a smooth production flow.

iv *Process layout.*   This is the type of layout, common with process work, where the technical aspects of production processes are the main layout determinants. Piping or ducts convey most of the material, and frequently successive operations are so integrated on automatic operation that the detailed layout becomes primarily a matter of engineering design. This does not mean that other arguments, such as maintenance access, become irrelevant, but the layout decision is subject to many more technical constraints, rather than detailed economic arguments.

b **Additional layout considerations**

Apart from the specific production aspects already discussed in Chapter Three, it will be convenient to summarize the other major factors that may be relevant to a layout decision. Some of these factors may already have been inferred from the previous discussion.

i Safety. Whatever the cost or production advantage, statutory requirements and common-law liability in respect of negligence make safety a basic consideration.

ii Production environment. Where it is necessary to provide a controlled environment for production, this is likely to affect the plant layout, such as in the case of the air-conditioned electronic production line mentioned in the previous section.

iii Personnel requirements. Human needs and welfare will require the provision of lockers, changing and wash rooms, all within convenient reach, adequate heating and ventilation, the segregation and control of nuisances. All these aspects affect layout thinking.

iv Supervision. Where the work is of a nature which makes close supervision important, the location of supervisory and technical staff and their offices, control rooms, etc, will require special consideration.

v Services. Where special services are required, such as a high-voltage electric supply to a heavy drive or a large volume of low-pressure air to chemical reaction vessels, the capital costs of such services become considerable and while long-service feeds may have to be accepted, the grouping of service users is often an important layout point in reducing both the cost and the complications of providing such a utility.

vi *Building aspects.* Particularly with existing buildings, attention has to be paid to floor loading, floor ducting, ceiling heights, gangways, stairs, lifts, lifting points, and fire escapes. Local byelaws are relevant here. In some industries production plant need not necessarily be under cover, as long as it can be suitably weather-proofed.

vii *Work in progress.* This is a general consideration, but is particularly relevant with batch production and a grouped layout approach. Where a number of operations have to be performed on an article in different sections, there is usually a queue of work waiting its turn on a given machine. Space has to be allotted for such work in progress within a production area as well as for inter-mediate and component stores, where parts are mar-shalled prior to assembly.

viii *Warehousing and transport.* The storage and prepara-tion for dispatch of finished goods can be a heavy floor-space claimant and the disposition of such areas in relation to the production departments is important. Loading and unloading points, turning and waiting areas for vehicles or railcars will also require considera-tion.

A number of other factors can also be cited, but these reflect more specialized situations. For instance, one com-pany was much influenced in making its production layout by the need to provide a good overall view from a visitor's gallery. This is unusual, but if a commercial context makes this an important advertising and sales promotion point and other considerations are regarded as less critical, then such a view may be justified.

REFERENCES

1 G. Terborgh: *Dynamic Equipment Policy*, McGraw-Hill, 1949.

FURTHER READING

E. Wilkinson: *Production Methods and Services*, Pitman, 1964.

Anglo-American Council on Productivity: *Plant Maintenance*, British Productivity Council, 1952.

O. Lyle: *The Efficient Use of Steam*, HMSO, 1963.

J. R. Immer: *Layout Planning Techniques*, McGraw-Hill, 1950.

DSIR (Building Research Station): *Factory Building Studies No. 1–12*, HMSO.

CHAPTER SEVEN

The Organization of Production

So far this book has been concerned with production in a preparatory sense. It has described what is involved in the development of a new product and the planning of the appropriate manufacturing facilities and works services. We are now interested in production as a going concern. If we were to take an instant picture of an engineering factory in full operation, we would wish to know, for example, why 'Job 5653/4' was on drilling machine X 146, in 'B' shop, or why 'Job 6165/9' was waiting for heat treatment, although already considerably overdue on delivery, etc. In general, we shall be concerned with how work is passed through a production unit in order to satisfy an existing or potential customer. This may sound quite elementary if only a few items are considered, but if thousands of units are produced each week, involving, in turn, hundreds of parts each, and these are again divided into broad product categories with at best only partial interchangeability, then there is complexity with every prospect of confusion. It is unlikely that everything will ever work out precisely in line with intent, so our question is not how can such confusion be avoided but how can it be kept within manageable limits without undue overheads? How in fact can production proceed on a day-to-day basis in an orderly and economic manner?

The answer here is a system of production organization which is concerned with the determination of what work shall be done in a given period and how such intent is transcribed into performance. Such a system is usually referred to as 'production control', and in practice many larger factories have a production-control manager, accountable for such a function. Most of the books on production control are tempted to take a wider interpretation, and they include material which comes more appropriately under production planning or quality control. In this context, production control refers to the scheduling of production commitments, as derived from the sales forecast or order book, to the determination of work priorities, the control of stock levels, the achievement of production programmes, and the effective use of working equipment. Production control differs from production planning in our approach, in so far as planning work incorporates primarily technological responsibilities and is normally performed by personnel capable of making technical decisions. Responsibility for the production-control function is in administrative terms, and while an appropriate technical background is always of help, there is no requirement for technological effectiveness. In practice, despite an occasional overlap, there is considerable difference between the bulk of personnel in the production planning and control departments in terms of training, qualifications, experience, and salary received.

If the broad purpose of production control is to establish and to achieve production programmes, then it can be anticipated that the technological setting in which such production takes place will have some influence on the nature of the production-control system that is installed. This is borne out in practice: while the basic objectives and principles remain similar, the precise systems that are in use can show wide variation. Production control is an answer to a particular organizational need. Most businesses have some specific requirements which differentiates them and their needs, and as a successful production-control system is essentially 'tailor made' to fit the situation that calls for it, variations can be expected. Consider, for instance, the difference between the manufacture of one standard brand of beer and the assembly of a large modern jet passenger airliner. In one case production control, as defined, may be a very modest activity; in the other it is a major undertaking, with a senior manager in charge. The ultimate objectives with both remain the same.

What is important, irrespective of precise form, is that a proper evaluation of production-control requirements is first made in the given context, ie, there is a need for proper systems analysis. When the needs have been established and defined, then an appropriate system can be developed and installed, bearing in mind the type of personnel that has to make a success of it in actual operation.

1 THE PRODUCTION-CONTROL FUNCTION

As the very name implies, production control is a facet of the overall responsibility for production. The manager responsible for this is normally the works manager or the production manager. Where the scale warrants it – and let us presume such a case – the production-control manager, in his role, will be accountable to the production or works manager for the effectiveness of the production-control function. By the very nature of his role, he will be a close colleague to the various line or departmental managers in production. In turn, he will have a number of sections responsible to him, and a typical illustration of his span of control in a large engineering works is indicated in Fig. 14.

In the broader works setting the production-control manager and his subordinates will work closely with the sales department, because the basic data for production programmes will come from there. In turn, the developed production schedules, or the relevant constituents, will go to the purchasing section, which will have to make corresponding supply arrangements, the production-planning section, plant department, cost accounts, etc. Production control has an integrating and coordinating purpose. It harnesses and dovetails both line and staff contributions so that the basic production programme will be achieved.

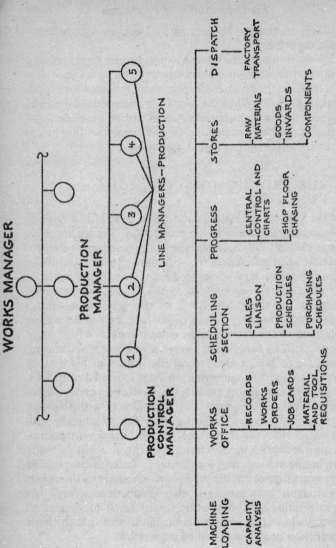

Fig. 14 TYPICAL PRODUCTION-CONTROL ORGANIZATION (LARGE ENGINEERING WORKS)

2 PRODUCTION SCHEDULING

Whether a company manufactures against stock (in anticipation of sale) or against firm customer orders, the basic initial data must be furnished to the manufacturing unit before any schedules can be prepared. The simplest system, where manufacture is solely against orders, is for the sales department to give instructions to the works as soon as an order is received, or to send the works a copy of its order acknowledgement – which serves as an authorization to proceed. The production-control section in the factory duly enters the order received on its records, and the order joins the queue for work to be done. This is typical of the small jobbing shop or of small batch production. If the queue of work is appreciably longer than was originally implied in terms of delivery promises to the customer the feedback will duly follow – when the customer's goodwill has been lost!

Unfortunately, such situations are commonplace, and they reflect the lack of the first requisite of a good system of production control – close contact with the sales department. It is this department which has the task of looking after customer requirements – what? how many? when? – and it is by meeting such requirements that the business stays alive. Where production is in expectation of sale, such as with the mass production of consumer durables, the sales department has to furnish and to commit itself to sales forecasts which can be confirmed in terms of production schedules. To this end, a sales department may well draw upon specialists to apply various statistical techniques for more accurate forecasting, but the basic responsibility for the provision of such data remains theirs. In a global sense, of course, the whole system of budgetary control and the anticipated scale of production rests, in any case, on the sales forecast. It is within such a global context, and with the more detailed information available for a shorter period, that production schedules can be prepared in the light of sales requirements. Most companies using budgetary-control systems forecast their sales in broad product or model categories for a period of, say, twelve months. Within such an overall operating period forecasts are made and revised monthly. When a forecast is, say, three months away the forecast becomes a commitment and the production-scheduling section is furnished with its basic data.

The primary task of the scheduling section is to transcribe the sales schedules into manufacturing programmes. The call for each product unit is broken into assembly requirements and component lists. Where there are common parts, and this can be expected with some measure of standardization, these are totalled for longer component production runs. Thus, the total sales programme becomes a detailed assembly and components schedule for the next manufacturing period. But a production programme of this type is more than a multiplication of sales data. There may have to be allowances for wastage and scrap, spare-parts requirements, or batch-size adjustments for economic production runs. As the standard manufacturing and assembly times are known, the degree of capacity utilization or overload will be brought out at the scheduling stage. This is important advance information to production management, as it provides guidance on future manning requirements, overtime commitments, and general shop activity. For instance, if there is, for some reason, a substantial imbalance of work on various production lines some of the extra load may be contracted out.

The issue of production schedules forms the administrative signal for the detailed preparatory work that must be undertaken before effective production can commence. The overall production schedules are first transcribed into materials or bought-out component quantities and delivery times. Such transcription may be carried out by the scheduling section, as a standard procedure, or, alternatively, may be undertaken by the purchasing department. The transcribed purchasing schedule then becomes an authorization to buy. Similarly, the production schedules serve as a guide to the works office section responsible for the issue of individual works orders and allied instructions. The accounts department and budget section will receive appropriate copies for cost evaluation and budgetary-control purposes. Copies of the basic production schedules will also give relevant information to the works manager, plant department, production-engineering section, quality control, stores and dispatch section, and sales department, so that all who could be concerned with the coming production activities are acquainted with its requirements and its implications.

An associated, but rather more specialized aspect, is the general matching of production rates with a variable sales pattern, where manufacture is against warehouse stock orders. Here is an opportunity for the application of linear-programming techniques and inventory models, the tools of operational research. These tools can be used to find appropriate production schedules to minimize batch production costs, on the one hand, and keep stock levels within acceptable limits, allowing for variable lead times in production, etc. The overall balancing of output with sales in a flexible or even volatile market setting also involves general business direction and, as such, becomes a wider issue.

The production scheduling associated with more complex products, such as aircraft or ships, which have a much longer manufacturing period, presents another special situation. Although quantities are small, the total task sequence is much greater, and more technical background is required in the preparation of production schedules because of the complicated interrelationships of different manufacturing and assembly activities. Critical-path analysis and other scheduling aids are normally applied, and such scheduling activities are in many ways more akin to project-planning work. Such scheduling work is a marginal case in relation to our interpretation.

3 THE WORKS ORDER

The works order section, within the production-control department, follows the scheduling group in the system of work initiation, and for the execution of its tasks it has the use of two basic sets of data:

i The production schedules for the next manufacturing periods.

ii The basic production order sheets prepared by the production-planning department. (Described in Chapter Three.)

This combination of data enables the works order section to collate all quantitative, technical, and programme information on to one set of documents, which will then contain all that is necessary for the relevant work to be undertaken. One may be tempted to question the need for such document if the work task is already known to the operating sections and the production schedule has already all the quantities required. In fact, the more a production pattern is on a continuous mass production or process basis, the less need is there for such a special works order. Where, however, production is on a jobbing or batch basis, even where batches run into many thousands, and if there is considerable but only detailed product variation, then the works order, because of its explicit and explanatory nature as to what should be made, justifies its role.

a Purpose of the works order

A distinction can be made here between a manufacturing and an assembly order, but in essence their objectives are similar. Depending on the detailed design, the works order itself can fulfil a number of administrative functions, and these can be categorized conveniently as follows:

i *Command.* The works order serves as an instruction to carry out a given set of work tasks. As such it is a management instruction in so far as the system, which gives rise to the works order, is sanctioned by management. The agreed routine reflects the situation in which an impersonal instruction is given. There may be a formal authorization signature by a manager on the order, but usually there is no need for it. The order itself becomes a commitment to the production department which receives it.

ii *Authority.* The works order provides the authority on the strength of which the production departments obtain their raw material, tools, and appropriate consumables. Where wage incentive schemes are in operation, the order also permits the submission of 'credits' for bonus calculations. In such a broad sense, therefore, the works order authorizes the use of company resources, and its reference number is normally debited with the cost of such resources as they are consumed.

iii *Instruction.* The order, incorporating or making reference to the production-planning sheets, will thus give the precise information about the sequence of operations, machines, tools, jigs, and gauges to be used, speeds and feeds, etc; that is, everything which a competent supervisor or setter needs to know in order to proceed with the work to hand.

iv *Progress record.* The works order can be so devised, with entry spaces or detachable counterfoils, as to provide a dated case history about the progress of a work task. If the counterfoils, for instance, are posted, as part of a reporting system, to a central progress office an up-to-date picture of the general production situation can be obtained more readily, and this will facilitate effective production control.

v *Inspection and deficiency reports.* As the work proceeds through various production stages, inspection reports and quantity counts are suitably recorded. This provides data as to production losses or scrap rates, relating to each operation or production process. The final count of goods, passed to stores or dispatch, is reported to production control, which will arrange for rework or supplementary batches if the overall deficiency is above predetermined levels.

vi *Cost reports.* The accounts copy of the works order can be used for the determination of batch costs, taking due note of excess hours, materials, and deficiencies, as reported during the progress of the work. It can also be used, where applicable, for the computation of production bonuses. For such control purposes a job card often forms part of the works order, and on this all production periods are 'clocked in'.

b The concept of the works order

The works order is essentially a vehicle for action, for seeing that work is done, and this must be borne in mind with the design of such a document. The system of operation which it reflects needs to be studied, proved, and defined. When such a systems analysis has been carried out it will be possible to establish who should receive copies of the document or its counterfoils and for what purpose. The design of the document should be associated with agreed and written procedures. Much of the information that appears on such forms will be derived from production-planning sheets The main additions will be quantity and date columns and appropriate spaces for counts, inspection reports, and amendments, such as when orders have to be split or rectification work is required. There is no one given best document pattern; the works order is a means to an end, and such an end is a function of a specific production situation.

The actual printing and duplication of a works order, with all the relevant batch quantities, etc, together with associated tags, job cards, and counterfoils, can be carried out in a number of proprietary ways. The physical strength or protection of the document is no small point, bearing in mind the total length of some production periods and the places to which the work and its covering order may at times have to be taken.

4 FOLLOW-UP AND CONTROL

It is a comforting feeling to know that all works orders for a production programme have been issued and the necessary data supplied. It is then up to the various production departments to carry on with their work, and the responsibility is on their shoulders if, for some reason, production programmes are not met. However, such a departmental view does not help the manufacturing unit as a whole. While there is no doubt about the reponsibility of the line management of production for the execution of agreed and accepted work schedules, the assistance of a progress section can still be of great value. The purpose of such section is to resolve detailed organizational obstacles which may prevent the achievement of production targets. Such difficulties are again more typical of engineering industries, on batch production and with grouped layout, where the progress of work and its movement from one section to another can meet a range of unexpected delays.

A progress section provides a functional staff service to production superintendents and section heads, in assisting with the flow of materials, components, drawings, and tools, where for some reason their delay may threaten the progress of production. This is particularly so in a large factory, where, in the pursuance of such tasks, line supervisors would otherwise spend too much time away from the sections which they control.

Furthermore, there is the risk of the departmental production view becoming misaligned with overall production needs, and it is one of the functions of a progress section to prevent this from becoming too serious. For instance, there is little glory in achieving production records on component manufacture when there are already ample stocks for the next assembly schedules, while one or two key items are running short and threaten a stoppage. There is a human preference, where choice exists, to do the work that is easier or more congenial, and this may be accentuated with a piece-work or other incentive scheme where wage payments are affected by the type of work handled. It is not only the payment aspect but the associated group work attitudes which affect the foreman's helpfulness with one job rather than another. It is a task of the progress section to assist with the overcoming of such resistances.

a **Progress reporting**

One of the tasks of a progress section is to collect all relevant information so that management can be provided at short notice with an overall picture of the state of production and the reasons for the particular position. It will also be able to furnish data on specific developments, such as the effect of a machine failure or the rejection of a batch of components. To enable the compilation of such information without too much work, standard systems of progress reporting can be devised. The appropriate data may come, in the first instance, from works order counterfoils, job or time cards, production-section work completion reports, inspection clearance, or dispatch notifications, etc. These are forwarded to a control and progress centre, where the information is entered on master progress sheets or on control charts.

There are several proprietary wall-chart systems, all with the basic feature of instant visual display of the current production situation – always provided the chart is kept up to date. When the works office issues its work orders, corresponding job tickets or cross references are entered on the chart. Where major stages of production can be segregated conveniently for control purposes, these may be suitably entered as individual or groups of operations, with appropriate time scales; alternatively, the global scheduled production period only may be shown. Such visual displays are essentially horizontal bar charts, with the length of each horizontal bar showing the scheduled production period on a calendar basis for each particular works order. The actual position, as against the scheduled intent, can be highlighted by a sliding cursor which is moved forward daily, or by a Gantt type of bar chart, where thin horizontal lines indicate the scheduled periods and corresponding thick lines, immediately underneath, show the actual duration of the work. Whatever the detail arrangement, colour system, or design of a wall chart or other means of display, it will be more useful if it highlights the tasks that are falling behind, rather than just show progress where this is in line with expectations. Production control, like management, can be more effective when it concentrates on deviations from established programmes.

An alternative approach to central progress reporting is

to transmit only delays, production rejects, or any other occurrence which jeopardizes production schedules. The concentration on and the visual display of such delays will focus attention on the most urgent tasks, and is therefore preferred by many production controllers. The routine data, for such an alternative approach, comes from stores shortage reports, inspection reject notes, etc.

b Progress chasing

This aspect of production control receives only modest attention in management literature, and perhaps this is due to the implied admission that the installed production-control system, for some reason or other, does not work quite as effectively as anticipated. One can appreciate the longing for the perfect system; one that catches every deviation, anticipates every trend, and eliminates every emergency. While there is some justification for the search for better organization, just as much as for better production processes, the law of diminishing returns nevertheless applies. There are economic limits in making production-control systems ever more ingenious, to catch every possible contingency and yet to expect the rank and file of humanity to operate them successfully. As the reader will note in section 6 of this chapter, computers and automation generally are beginning to make an impact on production control; but despite this, there are many cases where the on-the-spot investigation of an experienced progress chaser is most effective. There is a need in practice for a single-minded, flexible, tenacious, and resourceful individual to cut through misunderstandings and to stress priorities in a confused situation.

It is the object of the progress chaser to use his personal knowledge, skill, and resourcefulness to ensure, for his part, that production schedules can be kept. He will be more effective when, by intelligent anticipation, he avoids stoppages and losses of output, rather than to throw himself into emergency situations, once they have arisen, Where there is a threat of impending stoppage and he cannot personally correct the situation, it is his responsibility to report the appropriate facts in such a manner that their significance is quite clear. Progress chasing supplements progress reporting in so far as delays are taken up before they become serious and specific action on such developments is required. It is far less effective where there is no progress reporting and jobs become overdue before the chasing starts.

The term 'chasing' is quite fitting because often when a progress chaser looks for a job that is overdue it is quite often 'lost'. On batch production there is scope for the covering works order and its material to become separated, or for the material to be sent to the wrong department, where it stays, shunted, until someone begins to worry about it. Similarly, tools, gauges, and drawings, although ostensibly available from stores or drawing offices, are liable to be delayed or mislaid. It is not, however, the job of the progress chaser to tell the production supervisor how his operators should be assigned to priority tasks or how his section should be run. The giving of instructions to operators is a line management task; the progress chaser, as a functional staff man, may give advice and endeavour to persuade, but the final decision and associated responsibility rests with the manager concerned.

The detailed control and organization of progress chasing within a large factory may be on the basis of product lines or departments. It must be stressed, however, that progress chasing is a supplement to a reasonably effective production-control system; it is no substitute for it. Progress chasing itself must not get out of hand – there is a risk of favouritism when a number of progress chasers, for instance, compete for the attention of a specific production superintendent, and care must be taken that the vagaries of such human relationships do not obscure overall production requirements. Nor must the production supervisor feel that the progress of work does not concern him until the job is chased. An aid to effective production must not encroach on line-management responsibilities.

5 MACHINE LOADING

Where production takes place in a number of separate steps, involving different machines or processes, then a large number of priority alternatives could present themselves to the scheduling section when arranging a detailed works programme. The number of permutations can be visualized when taking, as an example, twenty different works orders which are routed to go through some or all of, say, eight work sections, with batch quantities, machine production rates, and setting times different in each case. With such a wide variety of competing work priorities, it will be important to establish some governing criteria to which these priorities could be ordered. These could be: minimum work in progress; minimum total work throughput time; minimum machine-work queues; long production runs; preference for certain bulk contract work; maximum overall machine-capacity utilization, etc. Each of these criteria will have its own optimum work priority arrangement, and it will be preferable, in the first instance, for one such criterion to be established as a standing term of reference, even if day-to-day commercial realities occasionally cut across it. The most common criterion is maximum capacity utilization. This is understandable – unused capacity is an asset that is not earning its keep, and an operator, standing idle by a machine for which there is no work, represents not only a financial loss but also a source of demoralization. The psychological appeal of seeing a works fully occupied, with a rhythm of ordered work movement, is an important consideration.

Machine loading involves the determination of the amount of work that has to be carried out by a particular machine. If, in a batch production shop, several different and competing batches have to be processed on that machine it includes the ordering of the queue of work that waits for the given operations to be carried out. Machine loading, in this sense, does not apply to the same degree where technical constraints require all work to go through the same machine or process anyway, provided there is sufficient overall production capacity. The usual situation reflects a choice between comparative, but not necessarily identical, machines, and the skill in machine loading is primarily associated with the balancing of a varied and variable work load with a given range of equipment and available work skills.

When the flow of production work comes in batches to a particular shop, say, a drilling and tapping section, the covering works order will specify either one particular drilling machine or a specific group of equipment to be used, with the final machine selection, where this is not technically critical, left, in such instances, to the section foreman. The production-control clerk, responsible for the area, then arranges the queue of work against the chosen machines. This can be done very conveniently in a graphical or chart form or with a proprietary machine-loading system. The use of any loading system is much enhanced when it is possible to see at a glance the amount of work outstanding on every machine and the time this will take to complete. It is therefore preferable to show particular batch commitments on a time scale, either in terms of standard hours or on a similar basis.

The value of a simple, but effective, machine-loading system is in its contribution to successful production management. Much of the benefit is already in the preparatory work, for when this is done properly it involves a specific mental exercise and an assessment of the implications of a particular production programme. Systematic machine-loading and work-queue analysis will give prompt indication of the degree of capacity overload or slack in a production department and will highlight plant bottlenecks. It will thus provide factual data on overtime or shift-work decisions, for machinery purchases and expansion projects. Work-completion promises become more useful when predictions are based on explicit analysis and the implications of priority changes can be more fully worked out. When an emergency arises, due to plant failure or rework, corresponding dispositions can be made more intelligently and without a general disruption of all other work.

The precise arrangements for, and the operation of, a machine-loading system can be suited to the general pattern of organization of a manufacturing plant. It could be centralized, with a section in the works office entirely responsible for the detailed loading programme for every item of equipment, or it could be developed on a sectional basis with the unit manager or foreman having staff assistance from the production-control department, where necessary. There is much in favour of decentralized operation – suitably coordinated – with a machine-loading system, as an aid to 'on the spot' management. As with all other organizational techniques, the justification is that the benefits provided exceed the work required for effective operation. The system should be simple and the information self-evident at a glance; flexibility is important, and the assumptions, on which machine loading is based, should have stood the test of experience.

6 PRODUCTION CONTROL BY COMPUTER

In recent years there has been a considerable increase in the number of computer applications to production control; and it is estimated that about 50 per cent of the computers sold in 1968 have had production control quoted as one of their primary applications. The trend is most marked in those companies which have already accumulated considerable electronic data-processing (EDP) experience, primarily on accounting records and general management-control information. Once computer applications had been proved and justified in these fields, it seemed logical to extend them to other promising functional areas, and here the great amount of detail, associated with production-control systems in large-scale manufacture, offered particular opportunities.

The computer is no golden elixir in solving production-control problems, and as in all its other fields of application, the installation of a computer system requires careful preparation and staff work. There is the need for a basic reappraisal and proper understanding of the production-control function. Why does the function exist in its particular form? What is required from it, and why? One can dismiss such questions as self-evident or elementary, but unless they are considered in the first place, much of the subsequent planning may be based on questionable assumptions. Production control must be evaluated both as a part of the overall and integrated manufacturing system and as a sub-system in its own right. Its definition may well affect other sub-systems, for example, inventory controls and purchasing procedures. It may also call for changes in the organizational structure of the manufacturing unit. Management and staff will have to participate in the analysis and planning of a computer-aided production-control system; a specialist system and programming section cannot devise its programmes in a vacuum. The implications of the coming change must be understood and its advantages patent to those concerned. The computer must be 'sold' as a production-control tool, with human and other organizational resistances minimized by a sensible system of communications.

The nature of the tasks that the computer can economically and effectively perform varies, of course, considerably with the corresponding manufacturing situation. It can be applied to mass production and assembly operations or unit and small batch work. The most frequent production-control tasks put on computers, disregarding for the moment associated operations such as wages analysis and labour-cost summaries, are as follows:

a *Preparation of manufacturing schedules.*   With the use of master parts and assembly lists, the computer can transcribe overall production requirements, as expressed by the sales forecast or order book, into detailed manufacturing schedules, covering every component or sub-assembly required. The master records are kept up to date by the incorporation of all design changes or detail modifications, so that their effect on production schedules becomes immediately apparent.

b *Preparation of purchasing and stores schedules.* These are further transcriptions of the manufacturing schedules, when the unit material requirements, as stated on the master engineering specifications, are collated and summarized for procurement purposes and stores issues. Where substantial inventories are already held, the computer stock record file can be used to establish net purchasing schedules.

c *Departmental-loading schedules.* Specific departmental work loads can be derived from the manufacturing schedules by the evaluation of unit standard operating times. Such data, which the computer can make readily available at the beginning of a production period, simplifies the disposition of production labour, the arrangement of possible overtime, etc.

d *Machine-loading programmes.* Particularly in the jobbing shop, where the different number of work batches and machining operations give a great number of alternative job sequences, the computer can derive the optimum sequence, with given parameters, to suit the desired criteria. It is also capable of rapid re-programming if an unexpected development requires changes in the work flow.

e *Critical-path analysis.* This is of importance in the manufacture of complex equipment, such as ships, aircraft, electronic equipment, etc, where actual product quantities are usually small but manufacture involves the marshalling of thousands of different components or assemblies drawn from within and from outside the company. There may also be a series of technical constraints which limit the flexibility of the assembly sequence. In those cases, especially where there are also many concurrent activities, the computer can determine the critical path of work, ie, that chain of tasks which will take the longest and which will therefore determine the overall manufacturing time. The computer can save

many man hours of planning time and quickly focus
management attention on the pace-setting constituents
of the overall manufacturing task.

f   Monitoring of production progress.   As work proceeds
and output is recorded, such data can be fed into the
computer, which can give an instant picture of the production situation and throw up variances in relation to
production schedules. Scrap and rectification work summaries can also be obtained.

It is now possible to put every machine in a workshop
on-line with a central control unit which automatically
counts each workpiece produced and records machine
downtime. Output details, productive time, and other
desired data are fed into the computer, which at the end of
each shift or week summarizes total production and
calculates efficiencies and utilization rates.

The computer in production control can offer clear
economic benefits, where it substantially reduces or eliminates routine clerical work. Its speed of operation and rate
of feedback can bring control into production situations
which hitherto proceeded on an *ad hoc* basis from one crisis
to the next. Alternatively, it allows greater flexibility and
variation in production operations which formerly were
thought administratively unmanageable. Its reliability and
ease of data storage provides new opportunities for production management to achieve more effective manufacturing
control.

The general, long-term benefits, although visible, may not
always be easy to quantify, and the actual worth of some of
the benefits claimed could well be questioned. It must be
appreciated that the computer is only a tool, and as such it
may be appropriate only for specific tasks. Where a computer
is installed specifically for the purpose of production control, it should not be exempt from the capital appraisal,
which relates net benefits to capital costs and obsolescence
rates.

ASSOCIATED ACTIVITIES

For the convenience of analysis, the discussion so far has been confined to production aspects. As, however, most production-control systems are a sub-section of the overall manufacturing organization, they can be used for the convenient collection of other data. The most common of such derivatives are given below, and these could equally apply to ordinary or computer-controlled systems.

Payroll data. This is normally based on a clock or time-card system, associated with works orders, and it is most common where there is a piece-work or other incentive scheme, linked with output.

Cost analysis. Particularly with batch or job production, the labour and material content, debited against a works order, can be costed and compared with estimates. This enables the compilation of overall cost records.

Stock records. The issue of materials and the booking in of completed work brings the production-control system close to inventory control. Stock records can be automatically updated in line with the production flow.

Dispatch statements. Where a company handles a large number of relatively low-value orders or shipments, dispatch instructions, shipment details, and invoices can be integrated with the works orders, and can contain all the data required for the completion of a given transaction. From this, sales and accounts summaries can be prepared and appropriate ledger entries made.

Work in progress measurement. A production-control system can readily furnish data as to the amount of work in progress and indicate the corresponding cash commitment involved.

Quality-control reports. These can be conveniently related to production schedules and highlight scrapped materials, quality trends, and rectification work.

Whatever the purpose of the associated activity, simple and time-saving transcription is, however, desirable, in the interest of administrative economy.

FURTHER READING

S. Eilon: *Elements of Production Planning and Control*, Macmillan, 1962.

K. G. Lockyer: *Production Control in Practice*, Pitman, 1966.

A. W. Willsmore: *Modern Production Control*, Pitman, 1963.

CHAPTER EIGHT

The Human Aspect of Production

A quick analysis of production and works-management appointments in the daily Press indicates the emphasis usually put by the advertising companies on previous 'responsible positions in charge of production' or on previous control of production labour. Compared to such basic line-management requirements, professional qualifications and experience are often at a discount to the company looking for the 'right man'. One may speculate on what is really wanted, but in substance, the quest is for the type of man who can successfully overcome the stresses of varied and complex relationships with subordinates, colleagues, and superiors; who can persuade a motley lot of human beings to work, contentedly if possible, on a number of diverse, but integrated, tasks and, in the end, still remain acceptable. Whatever else is required in addition, the need is for the executive who is aware of the human aspects of production and who can effectively deal with them.

Such a need is likely to continue because until there is a completely automatic factory, if ever, production performance will to some extent depend on human contributions. The manner in which people are handled and encouraged to make their contribution remains therefore important. The development of a high state of morale and good communications between management and men is relevant, sometimes even more relevant than minor improvements in production efficiency.

Human relations in industry furnish a popular subject

for platform speeches and management publications, and
if only 10 per cent of the proffered advice were taken one
might expect an industrial semi-paradise. In the profusion of
advice and discussion the lack of systematic knowledge
about the psychology of industrial relations, and its interplay with social and economic forces, is not fully appreciated,
and we have to turn to the historian to give us some indication as to why, at certain times in man's history, his record
of general achievement, viewed against the resources then
available, seems so remarkable. There seem tides in the
course of history which have galvanized groups of people;
provided a compelling motivation, a 'Dunkirk Spirit' perhaps, when achievement was outstanding, because people
responded. Such tides, however, are relatively infrequent; our
managers have to get results in a more pedestrian, less exciting
setting. The human climate inside a factory, although
capable of being changed for the better or the worse, reflects
a national or regional social environment. The skilful
practitioner will know how to build on it. Nevertheless,
political, economic, and social cross-currents will continue
to impinge on the social system represented by the manufacturing unit. Such a dynamic state of affairs, with its
perpetual need for adjustment, is not always welcome, particularly if, for instance, it comes in the form of government
prices and incomes legislation, which can completely change
industrial relationships.

The handling of human relations has to a great extent
remained an art, despite case-study teaching and role playing. While guidance can be given and training may improve
performance, the variability and complexity of relationships emphasize experience and proven skill. This has been
highlighted in periods of full employment and applies especially to industries which are labour intensive by nature.
Of course, this does not mean that just a flair for handling
people, as individuals or in groups, is sufficient. The modern
production manager must be familiar with social developments, he must understand the nature of personnel
work, the importance of training, the background of in-

lustrial bargaining, the role of trade unions, and the requirements of factory legislation, essentially conceived to safeguard work-people from the hazards of industrial operations.

HUMAN RELATIONSHIPS

The importance of human relationships is not confined to production situations; it permeates all aspects of functional management. However, as most industrial manpower is still associated with the manufacturing unit, an emphasis of human relationships is warranted in this context.

Some of the basic problems in this field stem from historical circumstances and their heritage of attitudes. For many years much of the bitterness of industrial relations has been ascribed to the long-term legacy of the Industrial Revolution. But times have changed, many lessons have been learned, we have a welfare state and unprecedented material prosperity. Is it because we are still preoccupied with the 'economic man', the 'rational decision-maker', who can order and maximize his satisfactions with Benthamite skill? We still judge in terms of the 'reasonable man' – as the law views him – rational, cautious, circumspect, conscious of, and freely entering into a contract of employment. When our concepts are shaken by wild-cat strikes, unofficial go-slows, and other manifestations of 'irrational' behaviour we blame the perversity of our age and sigh for the apparent orderliness of bygone years. Irrespective of our moral problems, as to what constitutes the right form of conduct, we need guidance from the behavioural scientist as to the forces which shape human behaviour and determine relationships.

a   The factory as a social system

Those who work in a factory constitute, collectively, a form of social community while they are together. Each and every one of its members imports a slice of his background, cultural environment, values, and personality when entering the work situation. The synthesis of all these varied contributions is not, however, their summation; a 'fermentation' takes place which reflects the interactions of the people who come together, and from this, informal groups will crystallize. The various groups will collectively develop a certain tone within the manufacturing establishment; Jaques, in his Tavistock Research work[1], refers here to the 'culture' of the factory. This does not, however, mean that everybody subscribes to it nor that every individual is accepted by a group. Nevertheless, a general tone emerges and interacts continuously with the behaviour of the group known officially or informally as 'management'. The patterns of behaviour, the attitudes, social values, and norms which become established reflect a most complicated interplay of human relationships, and it is important for a manager to appreciate this complexity in the first place. The formative influences on behaviour are unlikely to reflect simple cause-and-effect situations, and a study in depth will often be the requisite to fuller understanding. Much of the personal skill of a manager lies in the perception of the deeper influences rather than just surface manifestations and in allowing for these in his own behaviour.

b **The role of communications**

One major link, within any social system, is its means of communication. In the formal organizational context this covers the issue of instructions, the furnishing of reports, the development of procedures and systems, the handling and the retrieval of information, as well as much of the relations between colleagues, managers, and subordinates. In the informal sense, it simply describes the manner in which people can talk with each other and whether this is encouraged or hampered by the production environment. The whole edifice of modern industrial organization, based on the division of labour, presumes effective communications, and it is possible to relate group and general working effectiveness to its successful achievement. In this context, however, we are not primarily concerned with the formalized routines and procedures which reflect communications in an impersonal, mechanistic sense, but in the social framework, where he general climate and state of morale in a production plant mirrors the closeness between managers and the managed.

Communications, whether written or oral, are handicapped by the limitations of language. This is not only the inadequacy of words, even if well chosen, to convey the finer sense of a perceived situation but also the varied interpretations of, and the emotional associations with, language and the images thus conjured up in the mind of recipients. The language and address of an Oxford Union debate is miscast, when giving instructions at the coalface of a Scottish pit – even if the instruction is correct. It is common sense to approach people in a manner which is likely to evoke the desired response. Every communication or aspect of conduct of a manager is interpreted by a group in terms of its norms and attitudes – and these are not necessarily rational. Even silence can have its varied interpretations. The skilful production manager therefore is careful in the handling of communications, he anticipates the behaviour of those with whom he comes into contact and analyses the feedback from his communications to see whether they have achieved their objectives.

In a wider setting the extent to which factory management takes its labour force into its confidence is also important. To give broad indication of the policies of the company, its plans, its successes and problems, in a frank and objective manner is a positive contribution to good industrial relations. With this can be coupled the willingness or even encouragement to hear the views, fears, and suggestions of the people on the shop floor, either directly or through a representative system. In this manner good communications can ultimately point to the common interests of management and workpeople.

c **Job satisfaction**

We hear from time to time about successful businessmen and administrators who work twelve or more hours each day for long periods; who seem to love doing this and whose success is ascribed, to a large measure, to this 'discipline of hard work'. By contrast, the majority of our working population seems to be written off as 'clock watchers' – an implied condemnation, based on a presumed set of values. While we can and should readily acknowledge the great variations in human worth and apportion our esteem accordingly, we usually fail to inquire into the nature of the work involved and the impact of the physical as well as the psychological production environment on work attitudes.

The industrial engineer, and the work-study engineer in particular, is concerned with the effectiveness of working methods. His criteria are time, effort, and costs; understandably, the 'soul of man' does not concern him: it is outside his terms of reference. He reflects 'scientific management', he is a staff specialist, and, where appropriately applied, he has made a major contribution to industrial efficiency. Nobody denies the importance of this achievement, or the continuing need for his function. The social costs have not, however, been adequately appreciated. The industrial engineer, and the production technologist, have simplified working operations and deskilled them, complete tasks have been fragmented, work specifications have eliminated operator discretion. The sum total of these changes in the human context is known to the discerning production man. He is aware of the monotony and boredom of highly repetitive work; he knows some of the frustrations it can engender, the irrationality and fatigue that may come from it. Job enlargement – where this does not cut across efficiency – job rotation, music while you work, encouragement of gregariousness, reflect some management attempts to obtain greater work satisfaction or to provide at least a mental escape from the ever-present routine operation.

A deeper difficulty, referred to by Argyris[2], is the limited horizon available to the operator on fragmented routine operations. The work situation, particularly when completely preplanned, does not necessarily assist independent inquiry. With little knowledge of what else is going on, the fear of and the resistance to change is more marked. It is here where positive management and union attitudes and good communications can help.

d The scope for participation

There has been considerable public debate about the desirability of real industrial democracy, with worker participation in the affairs of the company, which provides the common livelihood. In practice, participation has been limited. Apart from the difficulty of defining what exactly is meant by participation, the problems of company law, dual responsibility, the access to and the safeguarding of confidential information, the delicacy of some commercial negotiations – all these and other factors have limited the growth of participation in overall management. Perhaps the greatest obstacle is the argument for clearly-defined management responsibility in running a business.

On the other hand, it may be held that the affairs of any social institution may be healthier if there is genuine involvement by the majority concerned. In this manner involvement could satisfy personal needs, such as the achievement of recognition and group acceptance. If such needs are given no expression, then there will be indifference and resistance, and some valuable resources may thus be lost to the business.

It is difficult, in the first instance, to see how these two conflicting concepts can be reconciled. It is not here a matter of ownership or nationalization; the problem is, how can the majority be given an opportunity to participate in the running of a complex organization which requires clear delineation of responsibilities, effective controls, and the appropriate managerial skills?

The opportunity lies in participation at the work-situation level which has a more concrete meaning to all concerned, and around which most of the work attitudes and tensions are built up. Without the sacrifice of sound technical judgement or advice, a skilled manager can stress the 'law of the situation' in his approach to problems. This pattern of observable and objective facts will often by itself already point to a given course of action. Managerial status and authority is discreet, not blatant; the emphasis is on leadership skill rather than hierarchical structure. A free discussion, a depersonalized situation, leads more easily to participation and the contribution of ideas. In the end it remains the manager's responsibility to make the appropriate decision, and he must be frank about such a responsibility. When properly expressed, it is unlikely to thwart participative discussion. The yield of such discussions will be the stimulus of ideas and even of latent conflict, the additional facts brought into the open, which would otherwise not have been appreciated, and the positive effect on personal relationships. The manager in production must, however, be helped by the sympathetic attitude and support of his own superiors; if the general setting is indifferent genuine participation may be quickly lost – the substitute of lip service is not worth having. The manager's skill of leadership and patience may be tested, and participative discussion may only be successful if a good deal of background information can be given.

Apart from the participative discussions on operational matters, there are specific aspects of a work situation which can be left to group discretion. For instance, the choice of colour schemes, when repainting, the arrangement of lockers, break periods, and related amenities – these are opportunities for self-determination and, where suitably taken, they can have a considerable effect on the general state of morale.

2   THE PERSONNEL FUNCTION

In a factory employing upwards of 400–500 people the line management of production normally has the assistance of a personnel department, to take over much of the detail work relating to employment. Such specialist work represents a staff activity and does not impinge on the control of personnel within the production manager's jurisdiction.

Where a factory's operational plans are developed, preferably on the basis of budgetary control, the anticipated work load can be transcribed conveniently into manning schedules. Just as the production manager will have the guidance of an operating budget, so his direct and indirect labour costs will reflect his manpower establishment for the period under review. Where the existing labour strength is below such requirements, he will be responsible for the initiating instructions to the personnel department. Such a manpower 'requisition' is, in practice, categorized into trade or job groups which have been developed either in line with established craft skills or on the basis of prior job analysis.

The line management of production is involved in job analysis and job description, which define the work tasks and responsibilities associated with a given post. Such work cannot be done in isolation by a personnel department. Without job descriptions, particularly for staff appointments, the line manager has no clear idea of what his subordinates are supposed to be doing, and for what they are being paid. Integral with a job description is the job specification, which details the range of training, experience, and abilities required by the holder of a given post. Job evaluation further dissects such job characteristics as the degree of skill required, nature of responsibility, extent of supervision, etc, and evaluates these on a rating or points scale for the purpose of salary grading. In essence, this establishes the worth of a given job in relation to a general salary structure. It also provides the basis for a merit-rating scheme and the assessment of performance.

The detailed tasks of the recruiting process are not of direct concern to the manager in production until it comes to the presentation of short-list candidates for the final selection. On the basis that any subordinate must be acceptable to his manager or supervisor, the manager has the responsibility for the final choice. Similarly, a manager, if in effective charge of his department, will have the ultimate decision as to who remains on his departmental payroll although, in practice, long-established company procedures and trade-union agreements on redundancy, have tended to narrow his discretion here.

While the institution of training programmes for apprentices, staff, or graduates has become a major part of the personnel function – often as a result of the Industrial Training Act 1964 – this in no way abrogates the responsibility of production management to ensure that its staff is properly trained. With the help of the personnel or training officer, a periodic staff review can suggest opportunities for developing the human resources available to a department. Their development is relevant in a dynamic business situation not only to make good the eventual staff wastage with time but also to provide, in a technical and manufacturing context, the reservoir of trained skill which enables a company to take and to digest future opportunities. Again, there is more to training than simply sending staff on external courses. The capacity and willingness to teach subordinates is one of the hallmarks of a good manager. The production environment itself provides many training opportunities, particularly for those with prospective careers in other departments whose only real contact with manufacturing is confined to a short training period. Training may also be specifically associated with impending promotion; for instance, the 'Training Within Industry for Supervisors' Scheme (TWI) was designed to meet the need for better-trained production supervisors and, with its stress on job instruction, job relations, and job methods, it provided a practical approach to better foremanship. Talent spotting and the development of management succession schemes has also become significant in some of the larger companies, and the production manager is getting increasingly involved with staff assistants on periods of job assignments. The handling of a potential élite and its integration with the day-to-day departmental situation is often no small matter.

In view of the numbers employed directly and indirectly on production, there is a close link between line management at various levels and the personnel department. There is also a tendency for line managers to become involved in associated extra-departmental activities, such as serving on selection or assessment committees, apprentice supervision, formulation and administration of work rules, membership of works councils, etc. Similarly, they will be concerned with welfare aspects, both in the immediate job context and the general employment sense.

3 PAY AND STATUS

Although it has been established by a number of investigations that the precise financial reward is by no means the dominant influence in many job attitudes, it forms a major aspect in employee relations, and often provides a focus for dissatisfactions arising from other causes.

The larger the company, the stronger is the urge to establish a comprehensive salaries and wages structure; the scale of administration favours simplification and a system which conserves managerial energy. There is, however, the associated risk, with such an overall wages scheme, that some finer aspects of work or changes in work pattern are not immediately recognized and are allowed to become a source of friction. Again, collective bargaining with the trade unions at national level, statutory minimum wages regulation under the Wages Councils Act 1959, and the 1968 Prices and Incomes Act have all in turn limited company discretion in such matters. Nevertheless, finer variations of the work situation in different companies, covered by the same national agreements, have given rise to work-place bargaining to secure supplementary payments, particularly where associated with incentive schemes. Such local agreements have subsequently become available as levers for general claims, irrespective of the context of the initial bargain. As a result we have what the Royal Commission on Trade Unions and Employers' Associations (The Donovan Report) 1965-8 describes as a chaotic wages position.

For the manual worker, earnings consist of basic or minimum wages to which may be added local increments or 'allowances', often depending on the supply and demand situation for particular crafts in the area. On top of these may be bonus earnings, based either on straight piece work or on a general incentive scheme. Finally, there is overtime, which in some industries has become so established and systematic as to make its pay a regular and essential constituent of the total weekly wage. Fringe benefits and emoluments in kind become more significant with staff, and often carry the complication of a status symbol.

A related development which is increasingly influencing labour relations is the growth of productivity bargaining. This is, in essence, a deal struck in the anticipation of a change in working practices. In return for a higher and usually consolidated time wage, workers are prepared to drop 'restrictive practices', such as the insistence on mates in certain craft trades, or be willing to accept the elimination of demarcation rules, which will permit the more flexible deployment of a labour force, particularly on maintenance work. The benefit to the company may come, firstly, in the reduction of overtime and general labour costs but may also be derived from smoother plant operation and fewer stoppages. The problems of negotiating effective productivity deals have been well documented by Flanders[3] in his account of the Fawley Agreements in 1960.

An aspect, close to pay, but not always in direct proportion with it, is status which reflects the position of the job holder within the factory community. Status can be expressed in terms of office accommodation, secretarial assistance, lunch facilities, and relative freedom from general factory rules, such as clocking in, timekeeping, etc. As it is a relative matter, differentials become significant and minor privileges focus attention. Status symbols can assume an importance within the social setting of the factory which seems disproportionate to the outsider; they reflect an amalgam of human aspirations and values, the synthesis of a specific culture. The broad division between the manual and white-collar worker in terms and conditions of employment has resulted in a dichotomy which does not necessarily reflect respective economic worth. Is it social progress when the chargehand fitter's daughter obtains staff status denied to her father just because she is a copy typist in a typing pool? This contrast in status has prompted several attempts, notably one by the Central Electricity Generating Board, to give staff status to all its workers. Such proposals have, however, been viewed so far by organized labour as a somewhat mixed package, and progress in this direction can at best only be described as modest.

4 LABOUR RELATIONS

The obvious is sometimes overlooked, it is too easily taken for granted – labour relations, for instance, are the summation and integration of human relationships. However, they acquire a new dimension when they are institutionalized, and in such a setting they form a complicated and contentious topic. The line manager in production cannot fail to be affected. He will be aware of the structure of collective bargaining and possibly be involved in the operation of negotiating machinery. He will appreciate that the formalized relationships, the rules and steps of formal procedure are qualified by the *de facto* situation on the shop floor. Unofficial, informal understandings (often misunderstandings) frequently supplant rather than supplement written agreement. This tenuous, unofficial world is nevertheless reality in many a decision context; unofficial strikes, which heavily outnumber the official ones, often stem from this source.

The history of the Trade Union Movement, the struggles and development of organized labour, throw light on present union attitudes and explain, at times, what looks incongruous or irrelevant at first glance. The role of the trade unions in achieving higher living standards for the working classes is somewhat taken for granted; the problems facing the unions are more readily noted. Unions are not exempt from the bureaucracy of large-scale organization. The two biggest trade unions, the Transport and General Workers'

Union and the Amalgamated Engineering and Foundry Workers' Union, now have a membership of over a million each, while two-thirds of all trade unionists are in the twenty biggest unions. Communications between the union executive and the rank and file is affected by distance and organization. Relative remoteness provides opportunities for unofficial, on-the-spot, movements where the close knowledge of a specific plant situation furnishes power to a local shop stewards' committee. Instead of taking the local initiative, the union is often entrained by events – which weakens discipline. Furthermore, technological changes have altered the industrial labour pattern; craft divisions and union representation do not reflect this. Despite the numerical predominance of the large unions, negotiation is complicated by the still considerable number of quite small unions. Defensive in relation to employers and the larger unions, they are sensitive about craft delineation and job demarcation; they stress the particularism of the labour scene. In view of the vulnerability of modern production plant to strike action by quite a small group of people, their bargaining power is often stronger than their total numbers would suggest.

The observant production manager will obtain many glimpses of trade-union activities in the day-to-day operation of his plant. He will be able to gauge the general attitude of workpeople to their trade unions and note the manner of decision-making on the shop floor or outside the factory gate. He will also become aware of the relations between trade unionists and those who refuse to join a union, particularly where the 'closed shop' is an issue. The election of shop stewards, the collection of dues, and the influence of outside bodies and events are also relevant.

The acceptance of organized labour within the industrial framework and the growth of governmental concern with industrial affairs, particularly as a result of the two world wars, has encouraged collective bargaining and joint negotiation. The impetus for formal joint consultation goes back to the report of the Whitley Committee, 1916–18, which recommended the establishment of joint industrial councils for each industry, consisting of representatives of employers and workpeople. Although by no means a substitute for direct contact between employers and trade unions, it was visualized that the councils would consider wages, hours, and working conditions for their industries, that they would establish or further develop machinery for the settlement of differences, concern themselves with the regularization of production and employment, determine industrial training requirements and deal with a number of related matters within their industry. Joint industrial councils are voluntary bodies, and they differ considerably in structure and effectiveness from industry to industry. Although the councils have had a varied history, they have made an overall contribution to the improvement of industrial relations and also acted as spokesmen for the industry as a whole, in relation to various government bodies and the outside world. In 1960 there were some 200 joint industrial councils in existence.

In those industries where there is no voluntary collective machinery to establish reasonable standards of remuneration the Wages Councils Act 1959 empowers the Ministry of Labour to establish wages councils by order. Such councils consist of representatives of workers and employers and may have independent outside members. The wages councils have power to fix minimum remuneration within their industries and may deal with such matters as holidays, holiday pay, waiting time, apprentices' pay, etc. There were about sixty such wages councils in 1960 covering about 3,500,000 workers[4].

The manager in production, although aware of such overall bodies and their influence, will often be more familiar with joint consultation at plant level. The works consultative committee (or its equivalent) is a forum which brings workers, staff, and management together for the discussion of matters of common concern. The committees are voluntary and normally advisory in character. The prerogative of management in the running of the business is accepted, but the opportunity is taken to obtain the views of workers' representatives on matters which affect workers and staff, such as changes in production processes, safety, welfare, work rules, etc. A channel of communication is also established for imparting the type of general company information which is preferably given face to face, and for receiving comments or grievances. Such consultative committees facilitate participation and can be a welcome contribution towards better plant relations. The precise role of a committee varies considerably, but it does not usually deal with matters of pay and working hours which are reserved for trade-union negotiation. The organization and proceedings can be quite local and informal, or they may be developed in detail, such as is the case with some of the nationalized industries. Works consultative committees have been a failure in some plants; in others they have enjoyed great success. Much depends here on managerial skill, the attitudes of both sides, and the general human climate within the plant.

5   FACTORY LEGISLATION AND SAFETY

The Chief Inspector of Factories, in his annual report for 1966, reported 296,610 industrial accidents and the death of 701 people as a result. Such statistics contain only the reported accidents, and it is estimated that there may well have been another 100,000 accidents which were not reported for one reason or another. Most of the accidents occurred in construction and production.

Apart from carelessness and the deliberate taking of unnecessary risks, many of the accidents arose from direct breaches of the Factories Act 1961. A competent production manager is familiar with the factory legislation, consolidated in this act, and which also empowers the Minister of Labour to make further special safety regulations. The Factories Act reflects the social concern with industrial working conditions, and this can be seen from its main subdivisions:

a *Safety.* This covers such aspects as the fencing and safeguarding of production plant, the safety of premises, hoists and lifts, cranes, floors, and passages, the provision of means of escape, safeguards against fire and explosion, the maintenance and inspection of boilers and air receivers, etc.

b *Health.* This regulates matters of cleanliness, overcrowding, ventilation, dust and fumes, lighting, drainage, sanitary conveniences. The special provisions relate to dangerous processes and to safeguards against industrial diseases.

c *Welfare.* The provisions here are concerned with the supply of drinking water, washing facilities, accommodation for clothing, sitting facilities, and first-aid.

d *Employment of Women and Young Persons.* The Act here is concerned with the working hours, rest intervals, overtime, holidays, and shift work for women and young persons, both under and over the age of sixteen.

e *Administration.* This is primarily associated with control and the enforcement of the Act, and includes such aspects as notice of occupation, posting of abstracts of the Act, maintenance of registers and the furnishing of returns, the appointment and duties of inspectors and doctors, rights of entry, and the reporting of accidents.

The five hundred or so factory inspectors concerned with the enforcement of the Act are also engaged in the general promotion of safe working practices above the minimum requirements of the law. In this role they give general safety guidance and comment on the design of safety equipment; specialists, such as the electrical and chemical inspectors, make a particular contribution where rapid technical change sometimes obscures long-term hazards.

Apart from the risks of prosecution, there is, of course, also the liability in common law, which requires a company to provide safe working conditions and to take reasonable care in the selection of fellow workers. Claims for damages, where accidents are due to negligence – and it is surprising how wide the stretch of the term 'negligence' can be in the Courts – may run well into five figures.

Managerial responsibility for manufacture includes the responsibility for safe working; the appointment of a full-time safety officer in large factories does not diminish the overall responsibility of line management. It is here, where the qualities of a manager as a leader and teacher have their scope. The attitude, the example, the enthusiasm of the manager for safety precautions are quickly noted and affect the general safety consciousness. Line supervision has an important role to play; the temptation to take short cuts when production or bonus earnings fall short must be resisted. Comprehensive training, insistence on the use of safety equipment and clothing, safety competitions, posters and records, all-round publicity, and a well-run safety committee – all can play their part in making the rank and file more safety conscious. In such efforts industrial management can enlist the aid of outside bodies such as the Royal Society for the Prevention of Accidents (ROSPA).

Technical progress will mean further contact with more dangerous and volatile materials, higher voltages, more radioactive substances. Tomorrow's risks are ahead of legislation; they are not always fully appreciated until some accident occurs. Continuous safe working is a challenge to progressive management.

REFERENCES

1   E. Jaques: *The Changing Culture of a Factory*, Tavistock Publications, 1951.
2   Argyris: *Personality and Organization*, Harper International Student Reprint, 1965.
3   A. Flanders: *The Fawley Productivity Agreements*, Faber, 1964.
4   Ministry of Labour: *Industrial Relations Handbook*, HMSO, 1961.

FURTHER READING

D. McGregor: *The Human Side of Enterprise*, McGraw-Hill, 1960.

C. H. Northcott: *Personnel Management*, Pitman, 1950.

W. French: *The Personnel Management Process*, Houghton, Mifflin Co, Boston, 1964.

CHAPTER NINE

The Management of Production

There are many facets to the management of production and its related activities. Management is involved in the planning and organization of production, quality control, maintenance systems, and all those basic operations which make a factory a going concern. It is, however, possible to separate from this range of concern those aspects of organization and control which are essentially administrative and part of the specific managerial responsibility. It is also necessary to differentiate in analysis between skill in administration and capacity for human relations. As the practice of management involves responsibility for the work of others, there is the tendency for the latter to get mixed up with the former. We have already spoken about product and production policies in Chapters Two and Three, and it is now proposed to stress in the production context and within expressed policies those managerial functions of organization, planning, staffing, coordination, and control, all of which are in some way interwoven with day-to-day production management.

1 ORGANIZATION

For the want of a better term, the word 'organization' is used here in a different sense to that in Chapter Seven, where it was applied to aspects of production control, in order to stress the non-technical character of that function. It is now used in the context of management and relates to the administrative structure of the production unit.

a The organizational structure

Imagine a sizeable factory, with a substantial production commitment, and forget all about the manner of the existing organization – presume you can make a fresh start. Such an exercise might be 'unthinkable' in practice; on the other hand, it clears the mind from the clutter of preconception. There will be a near instinctive urge to subdivide the total work content to make it more manageable; division of labour leads to functional specialization, and in this manner we see the emergence of major groups known as departments, such as quality control, the tool room, purchasing, etc. The volume of work may be such as to warrant further sub-functional specialization; for instance, the inspection work within the quality-control function may be divided into goods-inwards inspection, component inspection, and final product inspection – each quite distinct in the work carried out and the personnel employed. Organization establishes relationships between the different functions that express the various work needs, so as to integrate their specific contributions in the achievement of overall business objectives.

Furthermore, the multiplicity of tasks that have to be carried out can be arranged into appropriate groups, so that they can form the substance of a post or work role to which responsible staff can be appointed. In such a manner a large number of work roles can be established, but as soon as this happens, three major problems will arise:

i The need to issue instructions to the appointed staff. This will involve the provision of information and the authority to give orders. The first aspect will require an information system and established procedures – ie, the framework in which knowledge is collected, collated, and disseminated. The second reflects a managerial hierarchy, although this need not be essential in every case.

ii The need to control the work that is being carried out. This requires the initial setting of standards, targets, and budgets. The essence of a good control system is the quick indication of deviations that focus management attention on incipient developments.

iii The problem of coordination which arises because of misalignment between related work roles. Misalignment may be due to overlaps or gaps between adjoining work roles.

The important point here is to remember that such an analysis of work requirements and the consequent development of an organizational structure is not a once-for-all exercise. As the environment of the business alters, so the original organization structure may become increasingly out of line with changing needs. An organization structure is a means to an end. If it is sacrosanct, if it hampers adjustment in a changing world, then it becomes an obstacle rather than an aid to the success of the manufacturing undertaking. There will thus be a need for a periodic review of the organization structure.

The need for such a periodic adjustment of an organization structure to changes in business environment is regarded by some to be analogous to organic adaptation and, applying the biological concept of the evolutionary survival of the fittest, one might argue for maximum flexibility and the minimum structure, so as to facilitate response to changes in the outside world. While there may be some force in such an argument, in practice it is only the very smallest plants, operating largely on a personal basis, that can dispense with a formal structure. The informal give-and-take of a well-knitted team has its limitations in numbers and the individual personal characteristics it can handle.

Sound organization is confirmed by effectiveness in practice and while theoretical models can be developed and advocated, companies which have established successful organization structures have often started with a careful analysis of their business situation and then built on it, with a blend of practical experience and accepted principle. Joan Woodward, in her well-known study of manufacturing organizations in South-west Essex[1], noted the considerable variations in organization structure between different companies and related these to the manner of production, such as small batch, large batch, continuous production, and the associated technology. Admittedly, most manufacturing organizations have drawn on the classical concept of military or line structure and have associated this with functional specialization. The accepted synthesis of line and staff organization, with a line management, having direct authority and functional specialists, such as the industrial engineer, cost accountant, or plant electrical engineer, acting only in an advisory capacity and through line managers, represents, however, too one-sided a picture.

The concept of a manufacturing organization structure is frequently expressed in pyramid form and, for a given number of employees, the appropriate shape could be tall with a narrow base, as in Fig. 15, or short with a broad base, as shown in Fig. 16. The height of the pyramid reflects the various levels of authority, ie, the chain of command, while its width expresses the span of activities or sub-functions under the control of each respective level.

Woodward found that Fig. 15 was more frequently associated with engineering batch production while Fig. 16 was more typical of some process industries. The broad-base structure corresponded to capital-intensive production processes, which for their maintenance and development required a wide range of different technical contributions, often at professional level. The management of such production units involved more the coordination of different specialist skills rather than the direct control of a large labour force. The technical problems affecting the large integrated process plant have often such immediate repercussions on overall production that works management comes closer to the individual plant situation. Lines of communication are shortened and the number of intermediate levels kept down. Due to the variety and the advanced level of different technologies, the corresponding functional specialists have gained in strength in relation to line management, and where their technical recommendations are fused in committee, it requires a strong line manager to disregard or even to modify them. The 'Law of the Technical Situation' has become a potent force.

In contrast, where the range of production technology

CONCEPTS OF ORGANIZATIONAL STRUCTURE

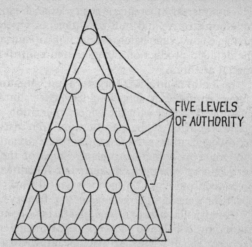

FIVE LEVELS
OF AUTHORITY

Fig. 15   LONG CHAIN OF COMMAND. NARROW
SPAN OF CONTROL

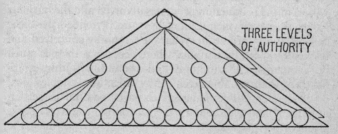

THREE LEVELS
OF AUTHORITY

Fig. 16   SHORT CHAIN OF COMMAND. WIDER
SPAN OF CONTROL

has remained fairly narrow, even despite perhaps considerable development within its practised span, the line manager, retaining a more detailed command of the technical situation, is more prominent in relation to staff specialists, particularly where the manpower within his jurisdiction figures more prominently than the capital assets employed. The number of different authority levels is more a function of administrative and staff requirements, especially in some of the engineering batch production organizations, where the detailed production planning and control tasks require special attention.

In both contrasting organization situations technical change continues to have long-term effects on line and staff relationships and, with the wider application of automated processes, there will be a greater need to recast our attitudes as to what will be the most appropriate organization structure for a manufacturing plant. Some of the interactions between line management and staff functions may be appreciated from Fig. 17, which is a typical works organization chart for a medium/large engineering factory.

A particular aspect of manufacturing organization is the autonomy which the local or departmental manager can exercise. This is particularly significant where a manufacturing group is geographically dispersed and the individual units are only of moderate size. A suitable balance between centralized control and 'on the spot discretion' must be found, and this balance may be substantially affected by the nature of the production processes involved and the business environment in which a plant operates. Provided the basic control and information systems are soundly conceived and backed by specialist support, where necessary, there is much in favour of local autonomy and discretion. Within established procedures, 'management by objectives' enables local or departmental line managers to participate in the setting of targets, and will commit them to strive towards agreed levels of performance.

Delegation in the context of production will permit quicker decision-making, which, for instance, in the field of

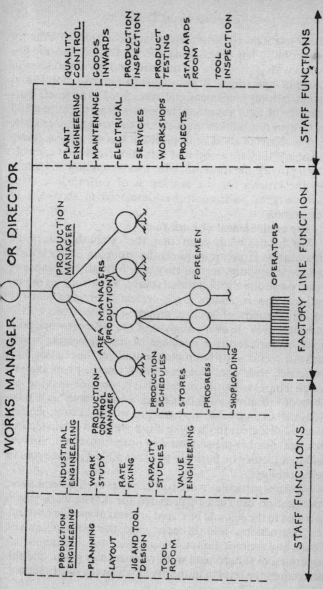

Fig. 17 TYPICAL WORKS ORGANIZATION CHART – MEDIUM/LARGE ENGINEERING FACTORY

labour relations, could anticipate incipient troubles. Primary responsibility has a seasoning effect on those who are entrusted with it; it makes for maturity and resourcefulness in charge of operations. It also tends to improve morale and harnesses local judgement and specialized experience. Furthermore, if local autonomy requires a department to stand on its own feet weaker units can be detected more quickly.

The benefits of decentralization are, of course, more valuable if they are associated with effective central controls which provide the framework for local discretion and establish the criteria for the evaluation of performance. This framework of basic control is developed in section 2 of this chapter.

b   **The establishment of work roles**

We have already seen that the establishment of an organization structure requires the grouping of work tasks and responsibilities so that they may form the substance of a post or position within the structure. While such an organizational apportionment is self-evident in practice, some of the implications of such a grouping are not too clearly understood. W. Brown's analysis of the different work positions in the executive structure of an engineering works makes a useful contribution to the study of the relationships associated with what he terms 'work roles'[2]. In an analysis which emphasizes the discretionary, decision-making aspects of executive work he defines a 'work role' as a position, within an executive system, to which decision-making work is allocated. In this way it is possible to subdivide in a practical manner the sum total of operational commitments within a factory or business to cover all levels and types of responsibility.

When a particular work role has thus been defined a role specification can then be prepared for it. The work that is ascribed to the role can be stated in terms of specific or standing instructions, and in each case the main objectives, limits, and areas of discretion can be defined. The immediate superior and subordinate work roles are also given, and this determines the level of authority at which the role functions.

Apart from the role of chief executive, there will be other roles at the same level of authority and, where required, appropriate lines of demarcation may be included in the specification, so as to integrate adjacent roles within the system as a whole. A concise title of appointment, an indication of the performance review mechanism, and an enumeration of special work aspects – such as the need for a certain amount of shift work – supplement the basic role specification. Once a particular role has been determined, that part of the organization structure has been defined.

It is important to remember here that the role analysis and the specification is part of the overall appraisal of the organizational structure and helps in the assessment of its appropriateness and relevance to the general business or factory situation. The structure is settled in terms of organization principles and not to suit the vagaries of human nature. However, arising from the basic role specification is the 'role requirement', which is a summary of the qualifications, qualities, experience, and abilities the holder of the role is expected to possess in order to succeed in his position. While the stress here is on such requirements, there may also be a concurrent indication of possible advance from this to more senior work roles. This helps in the planning of management succession where it is important for a company to visualize its managerial resources at various levels some years hence.

The full role specification although conceived in the context of organizational analysis, can serve as the basis for job description, job evaluation, and personnel recruitment, ie, it provides much of the data required for the normal exercise of the personnel function.

2 SYSTEMS

So far we have traced the establishment of an organization structure and the definition of its constituent parts, expressed in terms of role specifications. We have defined the accountability of the various work roles and established their formal relationships. It is as if we are in a theatre: the actors are on the stage, and they all have their parts; the play, however, has still to begin. The interrelationships of these parts, as expressed by the play, becomes now our concern.

Although the total work load is subdivided into individually manageable parts, no task is carried out in isolation. When we look at a manufacturing plant in normal operation we can observe groups of related activities which frequently cut across the functional or departmental subdivisions of the plant. Such groups of related tasks or activities are known as systems. They reflect a particular objective and are combined in a manner which permits its economic achievement. Thus a system of maintenance and overhaul of production plant interacts with production schedules, maintenance budgets, engineering labour control, spare-part inventories, etc. Routines and patterns of organization are evolved which harness related activities, as necessary, to achieve the particular objective of effective plant maintenance. We can thus ascribe to a system: objectives, a pattern of executive action or procedures, and a manner of self-regulation or control. Systems can be simple and local or complex, with a number of sub-systems integrated within an overall structure. In our context of the management of production we presume that systems will be deterministic, ie, a given instruction, within their context, will be certain to set off a known pattern of activities. This is not, of course, always the case in practice. We further simplify our analysis by assuming our systems to be 'closed'; no outside events impinge upon them, or at least their influence takes so long to make an impact that they can be neglected. Such an assumption is not necessarily unrealistic where a company has developed separate systems specifically to analyse and evaluate changes and trends in the outside world as part of, say, a management-services function, while the operational structure remains unchanged between periodic reviews or 'systems audits'. It will be noted that we confine our concept of systems here to the functional organization of a major business activity. We have excluded from this context the wider connotation of the word 'system', which to the social scientist also includes the larger framework of technical and social relationships, as may be found in an industrial community.

a **Planning activities**

We have already seen in Chapter Three that the process of planning is an integral part of the management of production. Indeed, without such prior planning, effective manufacture is unlikely to be achieved. It is a management responsibility to ensure the effectiveness of all planning activities, irrespective of the level at which these occur or whether the manager is personally involved or not. In the first instance this requires that those responsible for operational plans in a manufacturing plant are acquainted with the objectives and policies of the company in a context relevant to their situation. The setting of targets, be they in terms of production schedules or cost reduction, etc, furthermore, requires 'environmental information', the background data, in the context of which target decisions can be judged. A reasonably experienced subordinate can readily appraise a good part of his setting, but if his manager does not acquaint him with such relevant information as may come to him because of his role within the organization the judgement of the subordinate for the purpose of planning may be impaired. This does not mean, for instance, that confidential information can be freely disseminated, but if this forms an appreciable part of the planning situation, then some of the planning cannot be delegated beyond the limits of confidence.

In the context of economic analysis, planning activities concern themselves with the allocation of resources – in our case, to the processes of production. The benefit of sound planning is reflected here by the subsequent economy in the use of these resources, such as manpower, raw materials, fuel, etc. Furthermore, sound planning simplifies the establishment of operating controls as production proceeds. Yet in turn, planning activities can consume considerable resources themselves, particularly staff and managerial time. The economic advantage – in sum total – remains the criterion. Planning activities, too, can have diminishing returns; the cut-off point, where forward or detail planning becomes uneconomic, will be a function of given situations which may be difficult to quantify and may have to be resolved in the last resort by managerial judgement.

Apart from the overall and detailed planning of a specific manufacturing programme, the works or production manager will be concerned with other functional managers in a number of different planning tasks. For example, within budgetary-control systems he will become associated with financial planning. Similarly, he may be affected by, and be involved in, decisions on stock levels, as these can impinge on manufacturing economics, particularly with batch production and assembly operations. The following list is indicative of some of the planning activities which involve the management of production:

1 *Planning activities directly associated with production*
i   The determination of production processes.
ii The selection of production plant.
iii The measurement of work and the assessment of production capacity.
iv The arrangement and disposition of plant in terms of layout.
v   The functional and quantitative specification of plant services, such as gas, compressed air, electric power, etc.
vi The establishment of a quality-control system.
vii The specification of material-handling facilities.
viii The manning and organization of production units.
ix The scheduling of production work to meet sales forecasts or firm orders.

2 *Some general planning activities which affect production*
i   The development of payment and incentive schemes.
ii The training of foremen and supervisors.
iii The organization of maintenance programmes.
iv The planning of raw material purchasing schedules.
v   The establishment of cost-control procedures.

The nature of some planning activities, particularly at corporate level with large groups, has attained a high degree of sophistication. In such a context the manager responsible for production in a particular plant may be involved in the furnishing of data to a central services division and, in turn, use such services for specific planning activities, such as the installation of automatic stock controls or cost-reduction schemes. There is opportunity for the application of operational-research techniques, for simulation, the building of decision models, and systems design based on electronic data-processing. The success of such specialized planning activities is important to the operational performance of the manufacturing unit, and is therefore of direct concern to its management. The relationship between the management services unit, which is really an internal group of management consultants, and the line management of production, requires definition and may be best expressed on a client and professional service basis. The costs of such services should be charged on a realistic basis against the plants concerned and the achieved benefits quantified and related to them.

b **Control activities**

The great variety of tasks, the continuous use of resources, the commitments of the production unit, impose upon its management considerable problems of control. Without control, direction becomes meaningless and planning is a shadow exercise. The establishment and the periodic audit of control systems is a major managerial responsibility, and logically follows from its planning activities. Indeed, a separation of planning and control activities for the purpose of analysis is to some extent artificial, because even control systems require their own form of planning. For instance, the establishment of a particular budgetary-control system requires a good deal of forward investigation and planning if it is to achieve its objectives of financial control.

In our context, control is viewed as an act of supervision, checking, verification, and direction. It involves the comparison of performance with specific instructions, targets, or broad objectives, and includes the initiation of corrective action, where this is deemed necessary upon inquiry. It covers technical, organizational, financial, and human activities. In Fayol's view[3] control operates on everything; things, people, activities.

The broader aspects of control, with particular reference to systems, be they organizational, biological, or technological, have given birth to a new field of scientific inquiry – the subject of cybernetics. In its concern as to how social and organizational systems are controlled, it is of relevance to the management of production. One of the characteristics of a well-conceived control system is its capacity for self-regulation. Just as a numerically controlled machine tool can make its own adjustments upon the detection of a positional error, so it would be desirable in an organizational context to have a corresponding process of self-correction. The greater this degree of self-regulation, the more time will be available to managers, particularly at senior level, to develop new ideas and to investigate those opportunities which will affect the longer-term prospects of the business. Where the control system covers primarily routine work, the point of control should be organizationally as close to it as possible. In the manufacturing context, the foreman or unit manager will have such basic responsibility for on-the-spot control. With given work programmes and production schedules he will act as 'sensor'; he will note what goes on physically within his work section or appraise the data submitted to him by assistants. He becomes a 'discriminator' when he compares information, such as daily output figures, with the targets expressed in his production schedules. If the trend of production is within the forecast output range no action may be taken. Where, however, the deviation from the set standards is beyond anticipated limits, then corrective measures are taken, for example, in the form of a request for maintenance work to be carried out. The foreman has now turned into a 'decision-maker'.

Viewed from the level of the production manager, if there are a number of foremen, with their corresponding production sections, these will for the greater part of their work constitute local self-regulating systems or 'closed

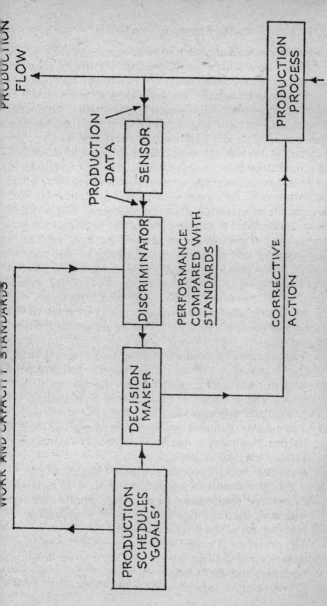

Fig. 18 CONTROL CYCLE. BASIC PRODUCTION SITUATION

loops', in control terms. From time to time problems will, however, arise which are beyond the control or terms of reference of the foremen, and their reports will constitute information to be handled or 'sensed' by a larger system at plant level, where the production manager will in turn act as sensor, discriminator, and decision-maker. This larger system will normally handle only those matters beyond the competence of the various subsidiary systems, and as such it will reflect the principle of 'management by exception'. In essence, line-manager resources are not frittered away where performance is consistent with targets or standards. Such a principle of exception does not, of course, rule out staff activities designed to improve production processes and performance. For instance, the production manager may head a committee on cost reduction which includes the cost accountant, a production technologist, industrial engineer, etc. But this has nothing to do with the function of control, even if effective systems of control facilitate such endeavours.

Managerial control of production units is expressed in a number of ways, of which the following are among the more important:

i The division of a production plant into cost centres and the establishment of operating budgets, to correspond with the activities carried out by the various departments. The provision of cost reports; their analysis and comparison with cost standards.

ii The manner of authorization of capital expenditure and the financial limits of discretion accorded to managers at various levels of authority.

iii Daily or weekly production and completion reports which give details of output, materials usages, labour efficiencies, rectification work, scrap reports, together with such control ratios as may be useful in judging the effectiveness of the production unit.

iv The provision of periodic labour analyses, giving details of direct and indirect labour hours and costs, lost time, overtime, and shift work.

v Quality control summaries.

Such methods of control often reflect standard documentation and procedures, and these may be extended in larger groups to operational and control handbooks which specify, within practical limits, a uniform system of managerial control. This, in turn, is frequently supplemented at a personal level by meetings between managers and supervisors of production. Again, control systems themselves may come under periodic scrutiny with 'internal audits' or system reviews.

It will be noted from the examples cited that control may start before the event in question, such as the need to obtain express authority for a particular capital expenditure. Alternatively, control may be concurrent with the activity, such as quality control or stock-level reporting, or it may be after the event, such as a review of the half-yearly manufacturing accounts.

The experienced manager will appreciate that every new development may not always be handled adequately by a given control system. Also, human beings are involved; judgement in apportionment and classification is required. The psychology of control is relevant: systems will affect the behaviour and relationships between controller and controlled. To the accountant, budgetary control is self-evident as an aid; to a hard-pressed departmental manager whose performance is at least in part judged by it, a budget may become a source of frustration. It is important that a control system accurately reflects the activities it endeavours to control, that deviations are quickly highlighted and prompt correction encouraged. Controls should be objective and flexible if necessary; they should be economical, easily understood, and be logical when related to the pattern of organization.

c Information flow

In our reference to planning and control activities we have inferred but not stressed the role of information which will be necessary for their proper exercise. The complexity of modern plant management has emphasized the need to evaluate the character of information flow as a major determinant of managerial effectiveness. In production there is a great range of decision-making, and this will call for information of many types; for instance, routine decisions may need only limited data on a predetermined basis. Thus it is relatively easy for a storekeeper to decide when to ask for replacement stock, given a specific stock figure and a re-order level. An information system can readily provide the framework for this sort of 'mechanistic' decision.

Where, however, decision-making involves judgement in the assessment of a number of alternatives, such as with the selection of new machinery or the development of a new production incentive scheme, then the flow and the character of the information required becomes much more complex. Where systems analysis defines appropriate decision areas for various levels and types of management – and this is important in our evaluation of managerial responsibility – then the flow of information must be tailored to suit. Such a design has to consider:

i That too much information is little better than insufficient information if it swamps the executive desk and detracts the manager from concentrating on the major issues for which he is responsible.

ii Information costs both time and money to prepare and to digest. It must in itself be subject to economic assessment.

iii Nevertheless, the quality, timing, and completeness of information has to be appropriate to the decisions that are expected from its scrutiny.

For a given role specification, such as 'Superintendent – Engine Assembly Shop', it will thus be possible to define the basic information required for the carrying out of this particular role. Information may come from outside, such as in the form of customer guarantee claims, or from within, as with engine completion summaries. Much of the information, particularly from outside, will be 'new' for each period of review, while other data, such as machine-capacity statements, are of a semi-permanent nature. Again, information may be complete in its account or it may be filtered, eg, a dispatch note where the invoice prices are blanked out.

To the manager, intent on improving the effectiveness of his plant, the flow of information is a basic concern.

d The role of the computer

We have already seen in Chapters Four and Seven that the computer is playing a growing part in the control of production processes and in the organization of production itself. The effectiveness of the computer in the context of production organization is, however, a function of the systems in which it operates. As a result, its introduction and scope for the handling, recording, storing, and processing of information has given some urgency to systems analysis and design. The concept of management information flow – right through the business – is beginning to influence organization structures. In many companies computer systems have already proved themselves in various functional tasks, eg, payroll accounting, stock control, production scheduling, etc. The trend is now towards the overall integration of all such activities. The speed at which information can be made available and processed strengthens central direction; geography is discounted in the multi-plant group, when data can be fed by direct line into a distant group computer. The impact of such developments on the various levels of management has yet to be fully appreciated.

REFERENCES

1 J. Woodward: *Industrial Organization: Theory and Practice*, Oxford University Press, 1965.
2 W. Brown: *Exploration in Management*, Heinemann, 1960.
3 H. Fayol: *General and Industrial Management*, Pitman, 1949.

FURTHER READING

H. Koontz and C. O'Donnell: *Principles of Management*, McGraw-Hill, 1964.
J. A. Litterer: *The Analysis of Organization*, Wiley, 1965.

CHAPTER TEN

The Economics of Production

While there are cases where manufacturing operations no longer constitute the major cost centre in an industrial concern, as with a heavily advertised mass-produced consumer article or item of toiletry, production, together with the procurement of raw materials, still remains the major expense in most industries. It is therefore important to ensure that production remains economic; apart perhaps from the occasional short-term fluctuation in business conditions. Except for such short-lived occurrences, production, in conjunction with sales, must generate a revenue in excess of all expenses incurred.

The economics of production are not, however, just a matter of effective operating management; they require the production unit to be appropriate in scale and structure to the markets which it serves.

1 THE SCALE OF PRODUCTION

The scale of production refers to the size and capacity of production units, not necessarily to the ramifications of the modern industrial corporation, which often contains a number of distinct businesses in their own commercial context. The ideal production capacity – or in the language of the economist, the optimum size of a production unit – is the one at which unit production costs are a minimum. This, of course, presumes a number of conditions, such as a corresponding level of demand, constant market prices, and a given state of technology. As the world around us is dynamic, some of these presumptions will be challenged before long, but this does not invalidate the economic analysis which is part of the overall planning task when sizing a production unit.

The determination of the scale of production is often used nowadays to demonstrate the concept of 'decision trees', ie, sequential decision-making. The process begins with a forecast of demand and the matching of this demand with appropriate production capacity. Unfortunately for the decision-maker, demand could be infinitely variable; the forecasts could be substantially out. If production capacity could be similarly variable in terms of investment and installation the problem would be somewhat reduced. But most production plant comes in discrete units and, while it need not necessarily be used to full capacity, its operating costs, allowing for depreciation, do not encourage partial use. Nevertheless, a commitment to a given production capacity is required, and this can be permutated against all levels of future demand. Each future demand situation can then lead to a number of 'second-stage' decisions, say one or two years hence when further extensions or a reduction of production capacity can be considered. In turn, each of the second-stage decisions can be visualized to lead to subsequent capacity decision situations in the more distant future. Such a large permutation of demand and capacity alternatives looks somewhat forbidding, but with a suitable computer programme this can become sufficiently manageable to be worth doing. From this a set tabulation or 'matrix' can be prepared, listing the nature and worth of all alternative scales of production and investment so that an appropriate and informed choice may be made.

The National Economic Development Office, in its 1967 review of British and American manpower practices in the chemical industries[1], stresses the cost advantage which the American chemical industry possesses because its basic production units are so much bigger than their British counterparts. No extra manpower is required for the operation of a valve on a 12-inch-diameter pipe instead of a 6-inch-diameter pipe; the tonnage flow, in broad terms, is, however, quadrupled, and the corresponding reduction in labour costs per unit output is self-evident.

There is a strong case for going to as large a scale of production as possible, always, of course, consistent with a level of acceptable risk. This is particularly so in the process industries, such as the chemical industry, food, pharmaceuticals, oil, etc, where the physical size of the installation and the costs of investments do not rise at the same rate as the production capacity of the plant. Typically, a plant handling 10,000 tons per annum may have a capital cost which is only about 40–50 per cent more than a similar unit of 5,000 tons capacity. Apart from the economy on capital account, there are, of course, a number of operating benefits, of which the following are among the most important:

i   Commercial opportunities for larger quantity discounts when buying raw material in bulk.

ii Greater justification for, and more economic use of, specialist staff.

iii Economies of scale in the provision of plant services, ie, steam, electric power, refrigerant, etc.

iv Better opportunities for the recovery of scrap or by-products.

There are also the possible benefits of longer production runs, such as when a large power station is on a base load, or the spreading of given overhead charges over a larger volume of output. Whether these benefits are in fact realized depends, however, also on factors outside the context of production.

The advantages of scale must not blind the planners to the measures of risk involved. Technical change can transform the mammoth plant into a dinosaur. The large and specialized production unit often lacks the flexibility which permits the modest but more general-purpose plant to survive.

2 FORMS OF PRODUCTION

It is common practice to classify different forms of production in terms of their economic character. The best known of these forms are: jobbing production, small-scale batch production, large-volume batch production, mass production, and process manufacture. The factors which determine the most appropriate form, in a particular situation, are primarily as follows:

i   The type of product and its particular characteristics. Consider, for instance, a bridge, a car, a bottle of detergent.

ii   The nature of the demand for the product; is it consistent or fickle? The size, permanence, and strength of the market is important. Much will depend on the repetition factor in production.

iii   The technical manner of production. Associated with this are such aspects as the product range to be handled, the degree of standardization feasible, and the qualities of material and workmanship required.

A JOBBING PRODUCTION

Jobbing production consists of the manufacture of one or several articles against specific customer requirements. In most cases it presumes the existence of a firm order against which the production commitment is entered. There is no expectation of a repeat order in the assessment of costs, and the quoted price normally includes all estimated expenses of design, engineering, and production preparation, such as the provision of special fixtures, etc. In some cases the customer is expected to pay explicitly for the tools and patterns that may be required if their cost is disproportionate to the value of the order. These tools could, in fact, remain the customer's property although kept on the supplier's premises. Jobbing production is typical of shipyard work, of contract precision machining, toolmaking, or the design and manufacture of specialist production plant. While the product may be of great complexity, accuracy, and refinement, the plant used to make it is usually of a general-purpose type. The production engineering design is much less developed than the product design itself, largely because of the difficulty of recovering such costs. Instead, much reliance is placed on a high level of craft skill on the shop floor, combined with technical resourcefulness at supervisor/chargehand level.

B BATCH PRODUCTION

Batch production exists where specific numbers of a given product are manufactured at various intervals, and where there is an expectation of similar further work. Batch production may be against firm orders or against stock in anticipation of sale. The former may be more frequent, where business is modest and orders are scattered, but as the scale of business and the number of orders begin to develop the latter may apply. There are no clean-cut lines between job and batch production at one end of the scale and between batch and mass production at the other end. Similarly, it would be difficult to establish precise divisions between small-scale and large-volume batch production.

The product is normally standard company design, although many permutations of accessories may be possible. One of the main features of batch production is that such product design and other preparation charges can be spread over a number of batches or comparative periods. Therefore it becomes worthwhile to give greater emphasis to the preplanning of production, to work study, layout analysis, production scheduling, jig and tool design, and the use of standard costs. It may also become economic to develop or to purchase specialist equipment. In the engineering industries batch production is often reflected by a grouped layout; it is preferable to keep similar plant, such as presses, in one area, with labour and supervision experienced in and concentrating on one type of production work. There is a greater division of labour, and this is reflected in the systems of control, procedures, and operating routines.

C MASS PRODUCTION

In this form of production there is the continuous output of standard or near standard goods, eg, cars, washing machines, television sets. Mass production is characterized by the complete pre-planning of all manufacturing processes and their integration in a flow process layout. Production plant is tailored, in detail, to manufacturing requirements and is either developed within the company or obtained from the appropriate specialist suppliers, who might be anywhere in the world. A small saving, in view of the large quantities involved, justifies substantial investment. Much attention is given to materials-handling systems, so as to reduce overall production times. Variety reduction is an important feature of mass production, and this could simplify production organization. However, the short-run inflexibility of a mass-production unit should be noted. Very careful inventory control is also necessary, because of the risk of a stock shortage stopping production, on the one hand, and substantial carrying charges, on the other. The variety of stock items that have to be held may, however, be less than in some batch-production plants.

In mass production division of labour, in both a functional and a work-task context, is taken to an unprecedented level. Because of this subdivision, most of the production work has become deskilled, and on some assembly lines people have become nearly as interchangeable as the components which they have to handle.

D PROCESS MANUFACTURE

Process manufacture covers those forms of production where powders, semi-solids, liquids, or gases constitute the substance of output. Production is mostly continuous, but can also be in a 'semi-continuous' or a batch form (beer, fine chemicals, etc). Perhaps the most distinguishing feature of such outputs is that they do not come in discrete units, but in a flow. The majority of process plant is designed to achieve production with a given process, and as a result such plant becomes relatively inflexible. Process manufacture is usually capital intensive; heavy investment in fixed assets is required, but as the plants are mostly on automatic or semi-automatic control, unit-production labour costs are usually modest. In fact, such labour costs may well be exceeded by depreciation charges, and sometimes even by royalty payments in respect of technical information or know-how'.

A particular aspect of investment here is also the relatively heavy expenditure on 'engineering charges', involved in the design, construction, and commissioning of large-scale process plants; an expenditure which is normally capitalized. A company may either instruct a specialist engineering firm to design and construct such plants or, alternatively, carry its own specialist engineering department, which can be a substantial commitment if it is to remain viable, irrespective of fluctuations in capital expenditure.

CAPACITY UTILIZATION

Once a commitment exists in respect of a given scale of production, there is a strong economic inducement to use the assets acquired to their full capacity. The greater the output over which depreciation charges and other fixed overheads can be spread, the lower will be the unit costs of production in accounting terms. Unfortunately, with variable market conditions full-capacity utilization is by no means assured, and this is usually taken into account by the more realistic type of investment calculation, which presumes a utilization rate of somewhat less than 100 per cent (either of a day shift or, with round-the-clock working, of a 24-hour day). The problem is: 'How much less than 100 per cent is acceptable?' Fig. 19 may help to answer this.

From Fig. 19 it will be obvious that if the volume of output drops below a given level, known as the 'break-even' point, the amount of turnover is insufficient to sustain the level of fixed and variable overheads. On the other hand, if output is well above such a point, then profits will increase quickly and at a much faster rate than the level of output. Much, therefore, will depend on the location of this break-even point in relation to full output. For capital-intensive industries the break-even point tends to be high, whereas with labour-intensive industries it could be relatively low.

Where a company is faced with a longer-term contraction of its markets, drastic reduction of fixed and variable overheads may be required; which could involve the reduction of staff and management, possibly the disposal of plant and

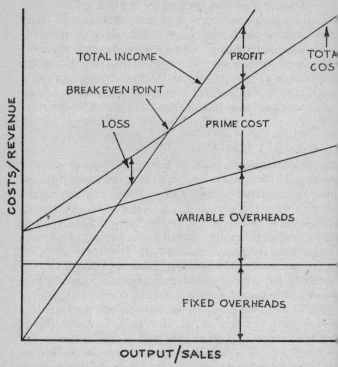

Fig. 19   SIMPLIFIED BREAK-EVEN CHART

the concentration of production in those factories able to operate at the lowest cost. This process of 'rationalization' is frequently associated with amalgamations in declining industries.

It should be noted that the straight lines shown in Fig. 19 are, for the purpose of illustration, a convenient simplification of a much more complicated situation. For example, costs are more likely to go up or down in steps rather than in neat straight lines.

4 ECONOMICS OF BATCH PRODUCTION

Batch production is a characteristic of many manufacturing industries, and although there may be great variations in batch size and frequency, these are nevertheless subject to common underlying economic arguments. Where a company manufactures only against firm orders, the batch size is largely set by the customer; but where manufacture is in anticipation of sale or against global forward schedules, then there is more discretion available to production management to determine 'optimum' batch sizes. The term 'optimum' needs some care in definition here. For instance, if we state that the optimum batch size is the one which is produced at the lowest unit cost, then we might stress the costs of production at the expense of the cost of subsequent storage and the commitment of working capital. Nor would this allow for the repercussions on an overall production programme if the optimum batch size for component 'A', with a given production capacity, multiplies the constraints on the production of components 'B' or 'C'.

Considering one specific batch only, the larger it is, the greater will be the number of units which can absorb the cost of setting up a machine. The main contributories to such costs are:

' The cost of skilled labour; such as the setters in the engineering industries who are responsible for the precision adjustments to tooling and machines. In some cases several man-days may be required for such work.

'i Machine idle time during the setting-up or, say, the wash-out period, when production runs are changed. The latter, for instance, is an important aspect of high-speed colour printing work on a batch basis.

ii Scrap and rectification work during the proving stage.

The higher the sum total of such expenses, the greater will be the pressure for longer runs. On the other hand, this also encourages further development work designed to reduce the costs of machine preparation and changeover. Thus in the engineering industries the presetting of tools is now more and more carried out away from the machine, and the resulting tool changeover, at a fraction of the former machine down time, has made a significant contribution to higher-capacity utilization.

The actual production operations, as distinct from the preparatory work, also furnish a number of arguments. A larger batch gains more from the operator's learning process, and a subsequent higher degree of skill may result in greater productivity, provided boredom and monotony have no significant effect on performance. This is particularly relevant with new operations and semi-prototype work. The technique of 'learning-curve analysis' endeavours to quantify in an analogous context such benefits of the learning process for the purpose of costing and estimating. Similarly, one can point to savings in material handling, material ordering, inspection times, etc.

Against the economic benefits of large batches, we must relate, with a given production capacity, the cost of work queues and the associated imbalance of production programmes which could affect delivery dates. Similarly, the ensuing inventory commitments must be costed. The reconciliation of such competing factors suggests the development of an operational-research model; and if there are many different batch-size alternatives, then a computer may be required for quick analysis. With the risks and costs of such complexity, however, there is a strong preference, in practice, for a simple set of decision rules, supplemented with a little resourcefulness, in case of trouble.

5   INVENTORY LEVELS

In its report and accounts for 1966, the Ford Motor Co Ltd, gave the following values in its group balance sheet:

Stocks	£96,900,000
Cash and Bank Balances	£1,900,000

The company's stocks were thus nearly 50 times the value of the cash balances, and presuming an interest rate of 8 per cent, which is modest in the present era of dear money, the financing charges in respect of these stocks were themselves four times the value of these cash balances. Alternatively, to visualize the scale of such costs, a carrying charge of about £8 million is equivalent to the employment of about 6,000 semi-skilled workers, which may cost the company about £1,300 per annum each, allowing for fringe benefits. While there may be some special factors in this particular case, there is no doubt as to the cost of carrying stocks, and even where inventory levels are more modest, they nevertheless constitute a significant resource commitment to the company concerned. As a result, many firms have strict limits on their stock levels, keeping them down to the equivalent of a few days' production.

The financial charges are not the only aspect involved. Many businesses would not have the physical space to house more than a limited amount of stock. With it also comes the risk of losses due to physical deterioration or the natural wastage of materials, such as with the evaporation of liquids. Precautions need to be taken against pilferage and the ingress of the elements. There is the further commitment in staff, floor space, lighting, and paperwork. Continuous vigilance is required to prevent the building up of obsolete stocks which have to be written off against the operating accounts.

In the context of production, stocks may be in raw-material form, part-finished goods or intermediates, components, and completed production held in anticipation of sale. There is also 'work in progress' which reflects the physical materials used in production or on the shop floor at any given moment, and which also allows for the added value of the production operations, so far completed. Except for finished stock, the other inventories are held to facilitate the smooth flow of production, but they may also reflect commercial opportunities for quantity discounts or well-timed buying.

Given, then, a production context and maximum permissible stock levels, it is important to know when to replenish stocks and what quantities to order. This depends primarily on the following:

i The time taken from the issue of the order to the receipt of the goods called for. This is known as the 'lead time.

ii The rate at which the existing stocks are expected to be consumed. This could be at a similar, higher, or lower rate than previous experience.

iii The level of safety stocks required in case of accident or failure of supply. This depends largely on past experience, but could be affected by specific developments such as a threatened transport strike or industrial disputes with a major supplier.

These three major aspects can be readily appreciated in a graphical form, as indicated in Fig. 20.

The expected rate of consumption has important forecasting implications. Whenever possible, a simple, self-regulating system of stock control is preferred, but such a system will have to overcome the effects of short-term fluctuations, yet still respond to longer-term trends. This can be done by a number of 'smoothing techniques'. The previous consumption rates are expressed in a moving average form, with extra weighting for more recent periods if desired. Furthermore, the forecast for the previous period can be compared with the actual figures, and an allowance for forecast errors can be made. The error quantity is multiplied by a 'smoothing coefficient' and the product added to the new forecast. The values of such a coefficient are between 0 and 1, and it will be appreciated that the nearer the coefficient is to 1, the greater will be the allowance for the previous forecast error. Such a device permits variable sensitivity in a stock-control system, to allow for short-term fluctuations.

If the initiation of a replenishment order at the re-order level is to be devised as a routine task, then it is preferable to have standard re-order quantities. Such quantities need

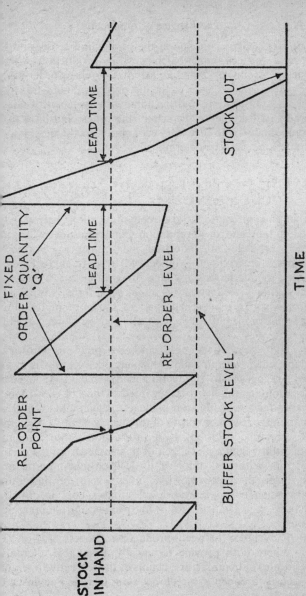

Fig. 20 TYPICAL STOCK-CONTROL GRAPH SHOWING VARIOUS USAGE PATTERNS

however, to be economic in the production sense, and t criteria for economic batch sizes in production will relevant. Similarly, when an external purchase order has be placed, factors, such as the discounts available, transpc facilities, inspection, and the administrative costs of raisi orders, will influence the size of the order, and have to compounded with inventory economics for the most appr priate lot size to be determined.

6 THE CONTRIBUTION OF MANAGEMEN ACCOUNTANCY

The gap in outlook and communication between t accountant and the production technologist is one of t great problems of industrial management. Schooled different environments, influenced by different value co cepts, their relationships lack integration, largely becau they know relatively little about each other's work a problems. This is perhaps part of the price of function specialization, but it could be reduced by closer acquai ance.

That component of accounting practice, known management accountancy, which includes costing, is of pa ticular concern to production management. Manageme accountancy ought to be regarded as one of the 'tools trade' for the production manager or technologist and n remain the sole prerogative of top management. The maki of economic decisions in a production context requir quantitative data, and much of this comes from the costi section. Without it the level of decision-making is reduc to inspired guesswork. (At times even the inspirati is missing!) The relevance of suitable cost informati may be seen from the following production planning ac vities:

i The choice between production process 'A' or 'I Where both provide technically acceptable alternati routes of manufacture, details of the respective operati costs become a major decision factor. For instanc the determination of hourly machining costs, allowing for capital charges, power, labour, etc, utilization rates achieved in practice, not just presumed – all this requires systematic cost analysis. If the total unit production times are known or can be derived synthetically from comparative data already available, then comparative production costs can be readily established.

The choice as to whether certain work should be contracted out to specialist firms or kept within the company. There again, the proposed contract prices have to be closely compared with the company's own costs. If the decision is affected by commercial or production policies and is made on criteria other than comparative costs, then the price paid for such policies can be quantified and debited against the advantages these policies are expected to have.

The technique of value analysis dissects the functions of a product and its components and evaluates the existing and the possible alternative ways of satisfying such functions. Technically feasible and functionally acceptable alternatives are ranked in order of costs, and a successful analysis will result in a cost reduction. The presumption underlying such an activity, and cost reduction generally, is the existence of an effective cost-information system. Without it, consistent reviews and improvements are handicapped, and one of the most important avenues, leading to manufacturing effectiveness, will be closed.

Management accountancy is a wide field of study, and tle more than its relevance to production can be mentioned here. The various costing methods, be they job, process, standard, or marginal costing, reflect, in essence, different production situations and the tools for operational control these call for. These methods, in turn, provide the basis for more sophisticated techniques, such as profit/volume ratios, inter-plant comparisons, etc. Again budgetary control is based on and closely associated with costing systems and expresses managerial control in financial terms. Acquaintance with management accountancy is requisite to the study of the economics of production in practical context.

7 THE ROLE OF OPERATIONAL RESEARCH

Where manufacture is on a substantial scale, with the commitment of commensurate resources, then there are increasing opportunities for the application of operational research techniques. Operational Research or its American counterpart, Operations Research, can perhaps be most suitably described by the definition adopted by the Operational Research Society:

'Operational research is the attack of modern science on complex problems arising in the direction and management of large systems of men, machines, materials, and money in industry, business, government and defence. The distinctive approach is to develop a scientific model of the system, incorporating measurements of factors such as chance and risk, with which to predict and compare the outcomes of alternative decisions, strategies or controls. The purpose is to help management to determine its policy and actions scientifically.'

This somewhat extended description stresses the need to quantify relevant factors, trends, or probabilities. The generalized statement that 'this or that may follow a decision' is regarded as insufficient: arguments must be quantified. In this respect, operational research has had an influence on the economic decisions within a business and, with its academic 'half-cousin', econometrics, it has also affected the study of economics itself. While there is much in favour of quantification and the building of mathematical models to simulate a particular business situation the presumptions and simplifications associated with quantification must be acknowledged. Particularly, the subjective assessment of risk requires care in enumeration; statistical data, reflecting past situations, may be misleading in the appraisal of new ventures, where the relevant experience comes after the commitment.

The first step in any operational-research task is a definition of the problem to be tackled and the criteria to be applied. This initial step is a salutary exercise, in its own right, for the process of diagnosis often brings out features in a situation which were not fully appreciated before. This is followed by the specification and the collection of the appropriate data and the building of a model, which is an expression of mathematical relationships. Solutions are obtained for the expressions thus established, and the model is subsequently tested for validity and completeness in the selected context. If the mathematically derived solutions are feasible in practice, then it becomes a matter of selling the findings to management, followed by the implementation of the resulting recommendations.

Some of the main fields of operational-research work, which have affected the economics of production, are as follows:

Linear programming techniques, applied particularly to machine-capacity studies, product blending, and analysis.

i Allocation of capital resources. Investment and replacement studies.

ii Production planning. Scheduling, shop loading, and operation-sequence analysis.

v Plant utilization; material-handling systems.

Inventory control.

i Queueing theory, with particular reference to work waiting at a machine point or operators waiting to be served at a tool or raw-material store.

ii Plant-failure analysis and preventive-maintenance systems.

REFERENCES

National Economic Development Office: *Manpower in the Chemical Industry: A Comparison of British and American Practices*, HMSO, 1967.

FURTHER READING

S. Eilon: *Elements of Production Planning and Control*, Macmillan, 1962.

J. Batty: *Management Accountancy*, MacDonald and Evans, 1963.

M. J. Sargeaunt: *Operational Research for Management*, Heinemann, 1965.

H. Dennett: *Unit Stock and Store Control*, Business Publications, 1963.

D. S. Davies, and M. C. McCarthy: *Introduction to Technological Economics*, Wiley, 1967.

CHAPTER ELEVEN

The Measurement of Production

There is no problem about the measurement of production. All that is required is the counting or weighing of whatever comes off at the far end of a production line. The problem only arises, but then in a substantial way, when outputs are related against expectations – against what ought to have been produced over the period in question; when the outputs are contrasted with the resources used, which in turn reflect the costs of production.

Where production plant is essentially automatic, measurement is simplified because such equipment is normally designed or bought against performance specifications. An acceptance test or commissioning run will verify the specifications or, alternatively, where the plant has difficulties in achieving them, it is still relatively straightforward, with appropriate instrumentation, to establish input feeds, outputs, and efficiencies at whatever level these may settle. It is when the human contribution is the prime factor influencing the rate of production, particularly with labour-intensive industries, that the problem of measurement becomes prominent.

WORK STUDY

It is the fundamental, the obvious question that is often ignored, either because we presume everyone knows the answer anyway, or there is the risk of being regarded as rather naïve when we ask about what is supposed to be self-evident. 'What should constitute a day's work?' The question was put explicitly by F. W. Taylor (1856–1915) the American pioneer of 'scientific management'. The endeavour to find a scientific, rather than a 'common-sense' answer to such a question was one of the main stimulant of the development of work study, which has now grown into the broader field of industrial engineering.

Work study, in the terms of British Standard Specification (BSS) No 3138, is a generic term for those techniques particularly method study and work measurement, which are used in the examination of human work in all its contexts, and which lead systematically to the investigation of all the factors affecting the efficiency and economy of the situation being reviewed in order to effect improvement. This concept indicates the relevance of work study to the management of production, for it is its systematic, scientific approach, with the intent to improvement, that can make material contribution to the effectiveness of a production unit. The main objectives of work study and industrial engineering are to achieve the most effective use of the input resources needed by the firm to achieve its output. Primarily this covers the labour, plant, and works services that have to be marshalled for the purpose of production. The evaluation of human work also provides the starting point for the objective determination of payment and incentive schemes. The role of work study is clearly reflected by, and will now be described in terms of, its two major constituents: method study and work measurement.

A METHOD STUDY

Method study is primarily concerned with the analysis of how work is done. To do this, a given task is broken into elements which are convenient for observation and study and each of these work elements is scrutinized in turn so as to attain the best practical working method. Again, to quote BSS 3138: 'Method study is the systematic recording and critical examination of existing and proposed ways of doing work, as a means of developing and applying easier and more effective methods and reducing costs.'

The first step in method study is to select work for analy

sis. Here we must remember that method study is a tool of management and that the use of tools constitutes an expense, which must be more than balanced by the gains of the study. Resultant benefit is the justification. Obviously, the work that is repetitive and substantial in labour content has a greater potential yield for method study than the occasional and somewhat marginal task.

Once the choice has been made, the process of observation and recording of the task begins, and here the method-study engineer can use well-established charting techniques such as:

i Outline-process charts. These charts describe with standard symbols the broad sequence of operations which constitute a process or manufacturing task. Reference to these has already been made in Chapter Three.

ii Flow-process charts. These are a more detailed description, using the same type of standard symbols, of the precise activities involved in a specific operation.

iii Multi-activity charts. These charts show in a bar form, to a common time scale, all the interrelated activities between one or several operators attending one or more machines. Such charts are valuable where 'team' or 'gang' work has to be analysed in a series of related tasks.

In this manner the facts about specific operations are established, with the information available in the detail form required. This permits the critical analysis of the various work-task components which may point to the elimination or combination of some of the task constituents. Such an examination considers the purpose, place, and sequence of the operation; who should carry it out and by what means. The best solution is, of course, the elimination of the work task altogether, but this may be a relatively infrequent experience. Failing this, the best possible method available in the circumstances is adopted. This may not be the 'ideal' method, but it is one which, in the given situation, is regarded as effective, reliable, economic, and safe. Such a devised method may entail a changed work layout, sometimes not only in respect of the particular but also the associated operations, or the provision of new fixtures, and such changes will have to be appraised in an economic context. Furthermore, new working methods have to be taught and maintained. The benefits of method study are only realized in the continued use of the better methods; a drift back to the former ways of working could nullify the efforts made.

Method study may be undertaken for its own sake or be associated with work measurement. It can secure improvements in work layout, production flow, and working conditions. Better design of equipment can reduce fatigue and improve the morale on the shop floor. These advantages may be well worth having, but in an economic sense they only have a real meaning if they can be quantified. This is the task of work measurement.

B WORK MEASUREMENT

Method study and work measurement are functionally the responsibility of a work-study department, and it is usual for the work-study engineer to carry out both tasks. Once the best practicable method has been installed and proved, work measurement is a logical next step; indeed, work measurement is implied already in method study, for the duration of the work task, even if only assessed rather than measured in detail, is an important economic criterion when comparing different working methods.

The substance of work measurement is reflected in the definition put forward by BSS No 3138:

'Work Measurement is the application of techniques, designed to establish the time for a qualified worker to carry out a specified job, at a defined level of performance.'

Where a work task is measured, the task constituents, defined by the method study, are further divided into elements. These consist of a series of well-defined movements suitable for measurement and sufficiently short in time to limit the number of variables involved. The duration of each element is recorded with a stop watch, and a number of times are obtained for the element under study. Concurrently, the observer assesses the effort a worker puts into his task, and a performance rating is obtained. An experienced work-study engineer can assess what is known as the 'standard rate of work', and will be able to give a quantitative judgement as to how much a given performance is either above or below this. Again, standard performance is defined by BSS No 3138 as:

> 'The rate of output which qualified workers will naturally achieve without over-exertion as an average over the working day or shift, provided they know and adhere to the specified method and provided they are motivated to apply themselves to their work.'

With a given number of performance ratings and element times, the work-study engineer will then establish the basic time for the element at the standard rate of work and by addition will obtain the basic time for all the elements of a production operation.

Where a substantial amount of work study has already been completed by a company, the accumulated experience becomes increasingly valuable for the purpose of predicting the standard time of a new but comparative operation. In fact, where the variations in a work task are primarily a function of component size which can change with different production batches, it may be convenient to take special studies from which the standard times of a whole range of product or component sizes can be derived for a specific work element. These studies can be expressed in a graphical or tabulated form, and the building up of such 'synthetic data' permits the derivation of basic times without the need for a special study. This reduces the cost of work measurement and makes standard times much more quickly available in respect of new work.

A more recent development has been the growth of Predetermined Motion Time Systems' (PMTS). These are proprietary systems which furnish standard elemental times in tabular form for various task constituents frequently found in a wide range of work. The times can be used for diverse industrial operations, and thus provide a yardstick for inter-industrial or inter-firm comparisons. They also facilitate estimating work at the design stage when no relevant production experience is available. In a successful application only a detailed operation analysis is required; the times can then be built up from the predetermined material available. Against such savings it will, however, be necessary to debit the cost of these systems, including the familiarization they require.

Where work is varied and rather limited in amount, it will be uneconomic to carry out detailed work measurement. A simplified approach, known as 'analytical estimating', uses established times for those work elements which are covered by synthetic data and estimates the remainder of the work. Much depends on the skill and experience of the estimator here, and a good deal can be learned from a comparison between the estimates times and the actual times taken when a job is complete. Analytical estimating is particularly useful for maintenance work in the process industries.

So far measurement has been concerned with the time an operation takes and with the level of performance achieved by the operator. Such a study is not, however, complete until provision is made for the onset of fatigue, personal needs, the cumulative effects of a given posture or motions, and for environmental factors. Man is not an automaton, neither in physical nor in physiological terms; the level of established performance must be one that can be maintained without excessive fatigue for the whole day or shift. Provision is made for such factors by the addition of relaxation allowances to the basic times already determined. These allowances are normally expressed in percentages, and vary with the type of work in question. They have nothing to do with the established breaks in working hours, but become part of the measured work cycle. This overall cycle time, consisting of the basic time and the relaxation allowances, is known as the 'standard time' for an operation.

Work measurement has become established in a wide range of industries, and has been accepted by employers and organized labour as a basic and relevant management technique. This acceptance has not been without its setbacks; work measurement, however objective and careful the approach, may imply a relationship that can easily become distasteful to the operator whose work is measured. It readily suggests to him the soullessness of the large corporation, the triumph of 'efficiency' and its presumption, in economic terms, on the purpose of work and life. Perhaps this feeling is reinforced by the growing proportion of indirect workers at clerical, technical, and managerial level whose performance is much more difficult to measure, and which as a result largely escapes detailed scrutiny. The present scope and challenge for work study is perhaps in the measurement of indirect work. But whatever the assignment, work study relies to a great extent for its success on sound human relationships within the factory.

2 PRODUCTION STUDIES

The purpose of such studies can perhaps be best appreciated in terms of the definition put forward by BSS No 3138:

'A Production Study is a continuous study of relatively lengthy duration, often extending over a period of one or more shifts, taken with the object of checking an existing or proposed standard time, or obtaining other information affecting the rate of output.'

The study involves continuous observation over a longer period of time than the normal time study, but is not as exacting in detailed analysis. It aims to reveal those job aspects that may not always be fully apparent where work study is carried out within a limited period, particularly where there is an unexplained pattern of lost output in relation to standard times. It permits further performance assessment, and thus provides a check on the ratings taken during the time study. Simultaneously, the observer can verify whether the installed working method is, in fact, used. Production studies may also be used where there is disagreement between the work-study engineer and shop stewards, especially when environmental factors become significant.

Where production studies are widely used, there can be substantial staff commitments. The information accumulates at a fast rate, and it becomes important to establish quickly what is worth further inquiry.

3 ACTIVITY SAMPLING

An alternative way of measuring production performance is provided by the technique of Activity Sampling. To establish what goes on in a production area, a number of instantaneous observations are made, at random, over a period of time of a group of machines, processes, or workers. Each observation records what is happening at that instant. The frequency of observations as a percentage, recorded for a particular activity or delay, will be a relative measure of time during which that activity or delay occurs. For a given number of observations the reliability of the results can be determined statistically, and the technique is equally suitable for measuring the work of direct labour, supervisory, service, and maintenance personnel. It can also be used for measuring the utilization of plant, equipment, space, vehicles, etc. In essence, Activity Sampling is such a flexible technique that it can be applied to a great variety of situations, provided the statistical aspects are clearly understood.

Where a high degree of accuracy is required, Activity Sampling is likely to become a very long-drawn-out business. In one particular survey of an assembly department employing about sixty operators, with twelve more classified as indirect labour, four experienced observers were required for ten working days. Another fifteen days of production study were then needed before the observers committed themselves to definite recommendations.

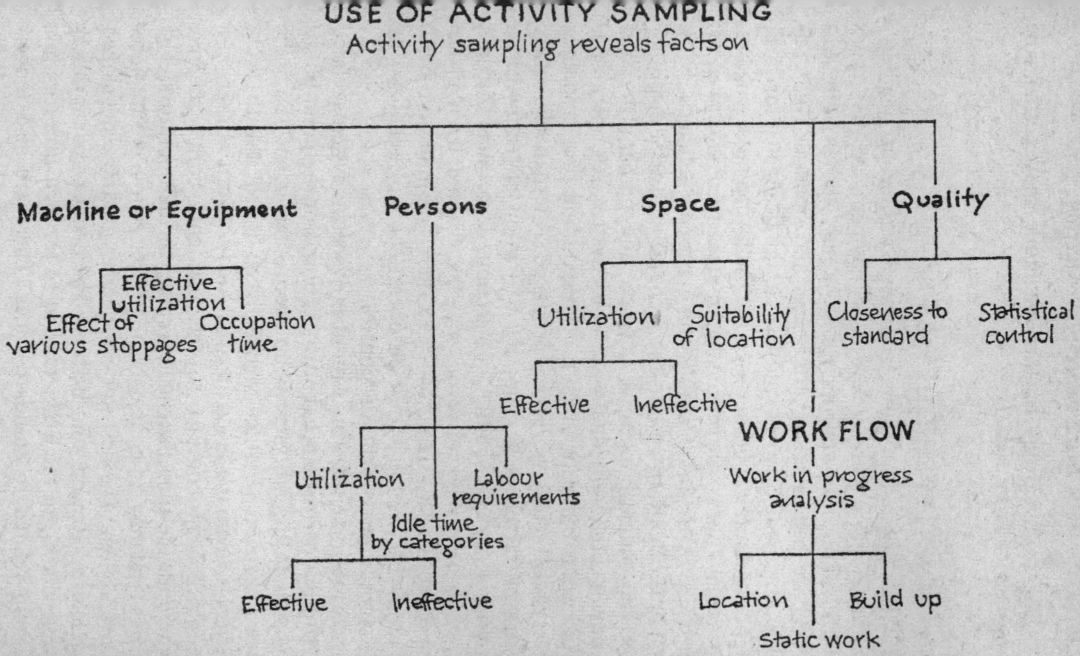

USE OF ACTIVITY SAMPLING

Activity sampling reveals factors on

Machine or Equipment

Effective Utilization
Effect of Occupation various stoppages time

Persons

Utilization
Idle time by categories
Labour requirements

Effective

Ineffective

Space

Utilization
Suitability of location

Effective

Ineffective

Quality

Closeness to standard
Statistical control

WORK FLOW

Work in progress analysis

Static work

Location

Build up

Fig. 21 THE APPLICATION OF ACTIVITY SAMPLING TO PRODUCTION

The ramifications of this technique may perhaps be appreciated from Fig. 21.

4 INCENTIVE SCHEMES

Taylor's original question, as to what was meant by a day's work, is particularly relevant to payment. A 'fair day's work' implied an appropriate day's pay, and as both concepts are bedevilled by arguments and opinions, the contribution made by work study was a significant step forward. Work measurement is at the root of many incentive schemes, although this by no means guarantees their effectiveness. Because of this association with payments schemes, work study is often thrown into the arena of industrial dispute.

The simplest incentive scheme, and perhaps the best known, is the individual piece-work system. An operator is paid a fixed sum or given a corresponding time credit for every satisfactory workpiece produced. Alternatively, where work effectiveness is primarily a function of teamwork, a group of operators, either in a section, department, or on a specific assembly conveyor, may be covered by a group piece-work system. In most cases there is a minimum basic wage level to ensure that an operator is not penalized by circumstances beyond his control.

In addition, there are a number of specific systems related to output performance, known as bonus or premium bonus systems. Although there is no precise agreement about the word 'premium', some writers have linked it with those schemes where the saved time is shared between workers and employers, in contrast to the 'straight' bonus scheme, where all the time benefit is credited to the operators. The latter type may, of course, come very close to a group piece-work system. The best known schemes are those developed by Halsey, Rowan, and Bedaux. The Bedaux system differs somewhat from the other two, in so far as it uses a points system related to standard times. There are also longer-term overall incentive schemes, such as the Scanlon Plan, based on global output, cost, and sales performance.

The great advantage of a well-designed incentive system is that it can bring about a higher output, and consequently lead to lower unit costs, with a given level of overheads. Supervision is simplified in some respects, as in the economic context, at least, worker and firm are integrated by a common objective. Unfortunately, however, not every system is well designed, nor is economic integration always enough. To the company, economic advantage is lessened if the clerical costs of computation become substantial and quality control has to be reinforced. Negotiations about rates can become protracted and may lead to sour relations on the shop floor. Where communications within a factory are defective and rumours prevalent, there could well be a restriction of output because of the fear (justified or not) that rates might be cut. Similarly, technical change may be resisted because of the opportunities this could provide for the retiming of an operation. Work allocation within a section may be affected by charges of favouritism, and the temptation to maximize payments rather than to meet a production schedule can lead to problems of production control in a batch-production plant.

Because of such difficulties there has been a swing away in some industries from the various incentive schemes towards 'measured day work' forms of payment. Work study is used to specify the rate of work required, and the standard times are used as the basis for capacity and cost calculations. Where the tempo of work is governed by machine or conveyor speeds, these are then adjusted to correspond to the specified standard output rates. Where an output incentive scheme is abandoned the new hourly rate is compounded from the previous piece-work earnings or similar, and it is normal for such consolidated earnings to be at least as high as with the previous scheme. The gains to production management are the greater flexibility of labour and a major reduction in negotiation and argument. On the other hand, high hourly time rates put a premium on the planning of work and an effective line management. It could be argued that this would be desirable anyway.

5 THE OVERALL EFFECTIVENESS OF A PRODUCTION UNIT

We have indicated in the previous sections that it is feasible to measure the performance of specific production lines or groups of operators. Most manufacturing plants, however, are composed of a number of such identifiable units, and while the summation of sectional performance evaluations is possible, this does not reflect very accurately the organization and use of all the resources available to those responsible for manufacturing operations. Typically, there can be great variations in the capital employed, both in fixed assets and working capital. Similarly, indirect labour, such as office staff, draughtsmen, storekeepers, computer programmers, systems analysts, etc, constitute resource use, and the effectiveness of their contribution to the total performance is equally relevant. Therefore if we wish to measure the effectiveness of overall production management our criteria must include all the varied resources to hand. This type of overall measurement is particularly valuable to the larger manufacturing group with a number of comparative, if not identical, plants in various locations.

The measurement of effectiveness broadly concerns itself with the relationships between resource inputs and product outputs. A few definitions may help to show what is involved: An *input* is defined here as the consumption of a particular resource in the process of production. This applies not only to raw materials but also to the equivalent time value of the work-study engineer who measures the operation or the production technologist who plans it. Similarly, it includes an appropriate amount of plant deterioration, which is a function of use. *Output*, in turn, is defined as the creation of goods and services. *Effectiveness* then becomes the ratio of outputs to inputs. Understandably, the endeavour is to maximize this ratio in economic terms. However, for a given level of technology, the ratio by itself has only limited practical value for the purpose of control. If, on the other hand, a specific ratio or standard of effectiveness is determined and then used as a target or standard, then we have a norm for the purpose of comparison, and we can talk in terms of *efficiency* in relation to the standard set.

The term 'productivity', so freely used in public discussion and exhortation, has been deliberately avoided. While broadly similar in concept, it has acquired many shades of meaning, which makes it somewhat less convenient for the purpose of analysis.

It is relatively simple to state and to measure certain inputs, such as direct and indirect production labour, consumables, and raw materials used. However, the measurement of resource inputs becomes much more difficult when we consider work with a large discretionary content, typically at managerial or professional level. There is also the complication of time apportionment when a particular executive deals with a number of products or several factories. Again we have the problem of plant deterioration, reflected by the consumption of capital values. The accounting concepts of depreciation may be only a partial guide; much depends on the manner of plant use and maintenance. Even on the output side there can be difficulties, particularly when part or most of the output is in services, such as with a laundry.

These complications are daunting, and may well discourage a firm from overall measurements. From a control aspect, however, it may not be that critical, if the original computation was somewhat artificial, provided it is subsequently used in a consistent manner and attention is primarily focused on trends. Nevertheless, a company may prefer the use of particular ratios or 'indicators' which reflect activities of specific concern. Such ratios can be conveniently divided into broad categories, relevant to production:

a **Use of resources**

This may include typical ratios such as:

Net added value per employee.

Net added value per direct production worker.

Net added value per 1,000 sq ft of floor area.

Machine running times related to available capacity.

Value of plant and machinery per direct worker, per employee.

Power consumption per direct worker.

Average age ratios of major plant and machinery.

Stocks per monthly net added value.

Work in progress per monthly net added value.

b **Cost relationships**

This, in turn, may suggest the following typical ratios:

Direct material costs related to output value.

Direct labour costs related to net added value.

Production overheads related to direct labour.

Central administration costs related to direct labour.

Indirect workers related to direct workers.

A great variety of ratios can be chosen, depending on what is of importance to a company in assessing the performance of its production plant. It will be noted that terms such as net added or output values have been used rather than sales figures. Admittedly, sales data may be more readily available and may make value terms look somewhat artificial. On the other hand, we are endeavouring to measure the effectiveness of production, not overall business success or marketing strategy. Where margins are eroded in competitive markets, the effectiveness of production will become more prominent, and it is helpful to have tools of analysis which focus more clearly on this.

Of course, the measurement of production is only one aspect of business appraisal. Marketing and financial ratios are of long standing, equally relevant, and are widely used. The opportunities for interfirm comparison, the use of operational-research and computing techniques have encouraged more quantitative forms of appraisal. While the case for market orientation is powerful, particularly in the consumer and consumer-durable industries, there are many fields of technological requirement where quality, performance, price, and prompt delivery are the major concern of a professional buyer. In such cases effectiveness of production – and the reputation for it – can provide the marginal advantage in the competitive situation.

In a fast-changing world a country with limited resources ignores such matters at its peril.

FURTHER READING

R. M. Currie: *Work Study*, Pitman, 1960.

M. J. Clay and B. H. Whalley: *Performance and Profitability*, Longmans, 1965.

D. Speed and P. H. Lowe: 'The Effectiveness of Production Units', *The Production Engineer*, August 1967.

Index

Index

MANAGEMENT SERIES

MANAGEMENT DECISION MAKING (30p) 6/-
A symposium of five international experts—British and American—stress the importance of scientific decision making in modern business administration.

MARKETING MANAGEMENT IN ACTION
(60p) 12/-
Victor P. Buell. A guide to successful marketing management by a former national vice-president of the American Marketing Association.

THE PRACTICE OF MANAGEMENT
($52\frac{1}{2}$p) 10/6
Peter F. Drucker. An outstanding contribution to management theory and practice.

MANAGING FOR RESULTS ($37\frac{1}{2}$p) 7/6
Peter F. Drucker. A 'what to do' book for the top echelons of management.

THE EFFECTIVE EXECUTIVE (35p) 7/-
Peter F. Drucker. How to develop the five talents essential to effectiveness and mould them into results by practical decision-making.

CYBERNETICS IN MANAGEMENT (40p) 8/-
F. H. George. Introduction to the ideas and methods used by cyberneticians in the running of modern business and government.

PLANNED MARKETING (30p) 6/-
Ralph Glasser. A lucid introduction to mid-Atlantic marketing techniques.

FINANCE AND ACCOUNTS FOR MANAGERS
(30p) 6/-
Desmond Goch. A vital and comprehensive guide to the understanding of financial problems in business.

BUSINESS PLANNING ($42\frac{1}{2}$p) 8/6
D. R. C. Halford. An absorbing and stimulating analysis of planning in all its faces.

INNOVATION IN MARKETING ($37\frac{1}{2}$p) 7/6
Theodore Levitt. A brilliant exposition of original and stimulating ideas on modern approaches to marketing.

MANAGEMENT SERIES (cont.)

THE ESSENCE OF PRODUCTION (40p) 8/-
P. H. Lowe. Explains the components, diversities and problems of production within the general framework of business management.

MAKING MANPOWER EFFECTIVE (Part 1)
(37½p) 7/6
James J. Lynch. The techniques of company manpower planning and forecasting.

SELLING AND SALESMANSHIP (25p) 5/-
R. G. Magnus-Hannaford. A clear, concise and forward looking exposition of practical principles and their application.

CAREERS IN MARKETING (30p) 6/-
An Institute of Marketing Review. A guide to those seeking a job in the exciting field of marketing.

THE PROPERTY BOOM (illus.) (37½p) 7/6
Oliver Marriott. The story of the personalities and the companies that emerged enriched from the commercial property industry in the years 1945-1965.

MARKETING (37½p) 7/6
Colin McIver. Includes chapters by Gordon Wilson on The Years of Revolution and Industrial Marketing.

EXPORTING: A Basic Guide to Selling Abroad
(37½p) 7/6
Robin Neillands and Henry Deschampsneufs. Shows how smaller and medium-sized companies can effectively obtain and develop overseas markets.

DYNAMIC BUSINESS MANAGEMENT
(25p) 5/-
Harold Norcross. A simple guide to the rudiments of successful business management.

FINANCIAL PLANNING AND CONTROL
(40p) 8/-
R. E. Palmer and A. H. Taylor. Explains the nature of the assistance which higher levels of accounting can provide in the planning and control of a modern business.

MANAGEMENT SERIES (cont.)

COMPUTERS FOR MANAGEMENT (30p) 6/-
Peter C. Sanderson. A timely appraisal of computers
and electronic data processing—their basic concepts,
potential and business application.

GUIDE TO SAMPLING (30p) 6/-
Morris James Slonim. A fine exposition of sampling
theory and techniques.

**MANAGEMENT INFORMATION—Its
Computation and Communication** (40p) 8/-
C. W. Smith, G. P. Mead, C. T. Wicks and G. A.
Yewdall. Discusses Education in Business Manage-
ment, Statistics for Business, Mathematics and
Computing, Operational Research, Communicating
Numerical Data.

THE REALITY OF MANAGEMENT (30p) 6/-
Rosemary Stewart. Compass bearings to help the
manager plot his career.

MANAGERS AND THEIR JOBS (35p) 7/-
Rosemary Stewart. Helps managers to analyse what
they can do, why they do it, and whether they can,
in fact, do it better.